THE BOOK OF THE DRAGON

**Dedicated to
all the extinct species.**

**'Man is clever enough
to obliterate a species
but has not,
as yet,
found a way of
re-creating one
that he has destroyed.'**

Gerald Durrell, *Catch Me a Colobus*

THE BOOK OF THE
DRAGON

CIRUELO

Text by
MONTSE SANT

Translation by ROS SCHWARTZ

Paper Tiger
An imprint of Dragon's World Ltd
Limpsfield
Surrey RH8 0DY
Great Britain

First published in Great Britain 1992
Reprinted 1993, 1994 (twice), 1995, 1996

The catalogue record for this book is available from the British Library.

ISBN 1 85028 214 5 (Limpback)
ISBN 1 85028 241 2 (Hardback)

Typeset by Bookworm Typesetting, Manchester, England
Quality printing and binding by
Amadeus S.p.A Rome Italy

CONTENTS

Introduction

This book is about dragons. Everybody knows what a dragon is: an enormous, fierce, bloodthirsty creature appearing in fairy tales and legends as an accessory whose main function is to set off the bravery of the knight challenging him. The dragon is an obscure, mysterious character, described only in broad terms, and is little more than a foil to enhance the hero's valour.

But the dragon is something else.

He is an admirable, intelligent and educated creature, who leads a most interesting life. He has some fascinating characteristics in addition to those occasional glimpses we are given through fairy tales and legends.

The aim of this book, written after long years of studying ancient manuscripts and patiently following the dragon's trail throughout the world, is to dispel the mystery surrounding these creatures, and draw the reader into a world which seems both within our grasp and beyond it.

You will find descriptions of the dragon's habits, customs and tastes, a catalogue of the different types of dragon, together with his physical attributes and patterns of existence. However, this book does not claim to be an encyclopedia of dragons or an exhaustive treaty on Dragon Science, for such a work would fill volumes.

We are trying purely to enter the secret world of the dragon, which is why this will be a useful book for everyone who admires and is interested in these beautiful beasts, while those who are not acquainted with their charms and qualities can discover and learn to appreciate them.

The dragon has always been slandered and misjudged, persecuted and hounded by man, simply because he is different. Like so many other living beings, he has experienced death and persecution in the name of the so-called superiority of civilized man.

Perhaps, in the future, man will learn that with the death of a single animal or plant species an irreplaceable asset – something more precious than all the wealth in the world – is lost. Only then will the Earth continue to be a brilliant blue jewel in the universe, for in its heart will be locked the priceless treasure of the diversity of the species, and man will have recognized his duty to cherish every single one.

Psychological Characteristics

The adult dragon is astute and powerful and sure of his strength. His cunning helps him elude the ingenious traps laid by man with a spirit that could be described as sporting. He is usually avaricious and fairly insolent, which is only to be expected given his power and considerable physical strength.

Dragons are very fond of jewels and precious stones, and they hoard treasure greedily. Perfect connoisseurs, they are discerning in their appreciation of gems, and it is not easy to deceive them as to a stone's value. They are lovers of conundrums, and often promise to set their victims free on condition that they find the answer to a riddle.

They are usually very proud and have an acute sense of ridicule. Nothing

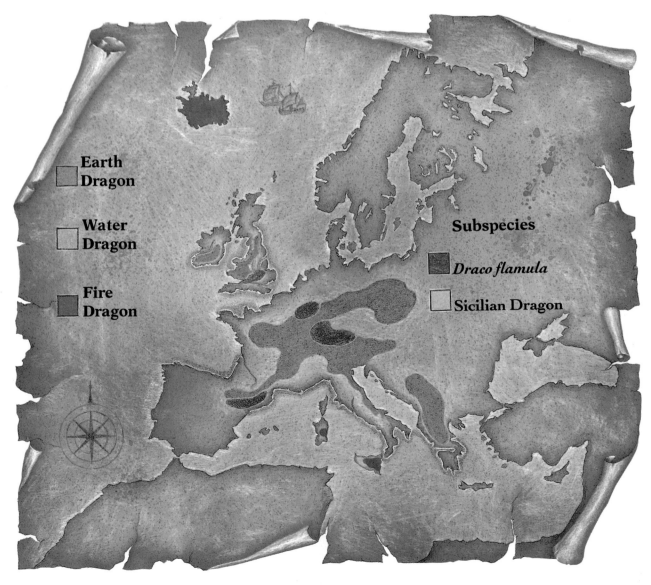

Earth Dragon

Water Dragon

Fire Dragon

Subspecies

Draco flamula

Sicilian Dragon

infuriates them more than being made fun of by humans. This is something we have to bear in mind when dealing with a dragon. If we embarrass him, he will retreat to his hide-out in shame and will refuse to have anything to do with us. But if we speak to him circumspectly, and show that we are capable of keeping his secrets, we will gain his confidence and achieve great influence over him.

The dragon is very well-versed in magic and knows the power associated with names. So important are they that the surest way to defeat and subdue him is to discover his name, which he keeps a closely-guarded secret.

The true name of a dragon is a synthesis of his personality and his history. It expresses his origin – it is important to note that dragon ancestry is transmitted via the father – and also by all that the dragon has achieved during his life, his aspirations, his knowledge and his level of mastery of magic. His name is usually conferred on him by his father at birth, but it is modified throughout his life. The secret is guarded so jealously that a dragon's real name is known only to the dragon himself and the Dragon Father.

The dragon also has one or several assumed names by which he is known. We would like to emphasize that out of respect for dragon practice, all the names used here are assumed names. For easy reference, we have grouped the dragons into three large families: **Earth Dragons, Water Dragons, Fire Dragons.**

Nuptial route taken by Water Dragons

Nuptial route taken by ordinary Dragons

11

General Comments and Physiology

The dragon *(Drago drago)* is a homoiothermic reptile. In other words, he is a warm-blooded creature and his body temperature is controlled internally. This characteristic enables him to adapt to the different climates of his very extensive habitat and to maintain his activities both day and night throughout the year, as he is not dependent on the warmth from the sun like the other reptiles. The dragon generally has wings, and his bones are hollow, for lightness. There are dragons, usually ancient survivors from the distant past, with stumpy legs and no wings. These rare survivors of a remote era are intelligent and fairly aggressive, and belong to a single species known as 'worms of the deep', a species on the verge of extinction. This creature lives for a very long time. There are records of dragons who have lived for five hundred and even a thousand years, but there are no known cases of dragons who have died from old age. On the other hand, they die from accidents, certain diseases, or as a result of the actions of their most relentless enemy: MAN.

They are susceptible to few illnesses, and the most serious threats vary from one family to another. In the case of the Fire Dragon, the worst disease is 'scale corrosion', which can be fatal. 'Senile dementia' is more common among Earth Dragons, while acute gastritis *non virginae* affects mainly the Water Dragon, who has an extremely delicate stomach.

Despite his strength, the dragon loses some of his agility with age, easily falling prey to the singular and terrible dragon-killer, the armour-plated *Ichneumon*. This swamp dweller, which Pliny describes in his *Historia Naturalis* as a spindle-shaped mud fish with a sharp snout, covered with tough plates, is the dragon's mortal enemy. The *Ichneumon* burrows between the dragon's scales and, using its sharp snout, tunnels through the tender flesh until it reaches the entrails, which it devours, killing its victim.

The dragon can talk, and his natural language is Latin, a tongue which is innate in the dragon species, but he has no difficulty in learning and expressing himself correctly in the vernacular of the region in which he lives.

A lover of woodlands and fresh air, the dragon cannot bear environmental pollution or the tumult of civilization. The only exception to this rule is a race of dragons, *Draco flamula*, which we will come to later. Today, the dragon survives only in those rare places that have escaped pollution, small isolated pockets of the Old World, which is why the future of the dragon seems precarious.

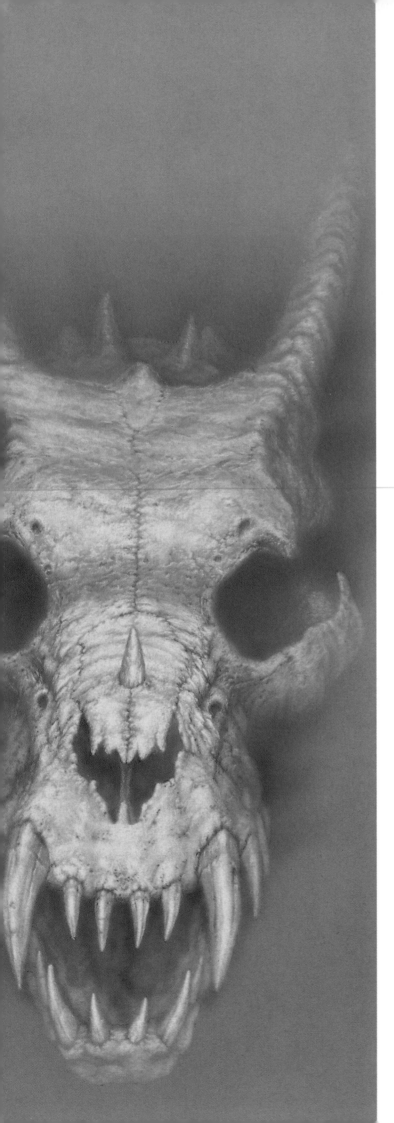

The Skeleton

T he dragon is the largest known
flying creature. To maintain his
enormous bulk in the air, his physical
structure has had to be different from
that of other reptiles.

His wing bones fit on to broad
shoulders which support the powerful
wing muscles; these require an
extraordinary articulatory system
unknown in other species.

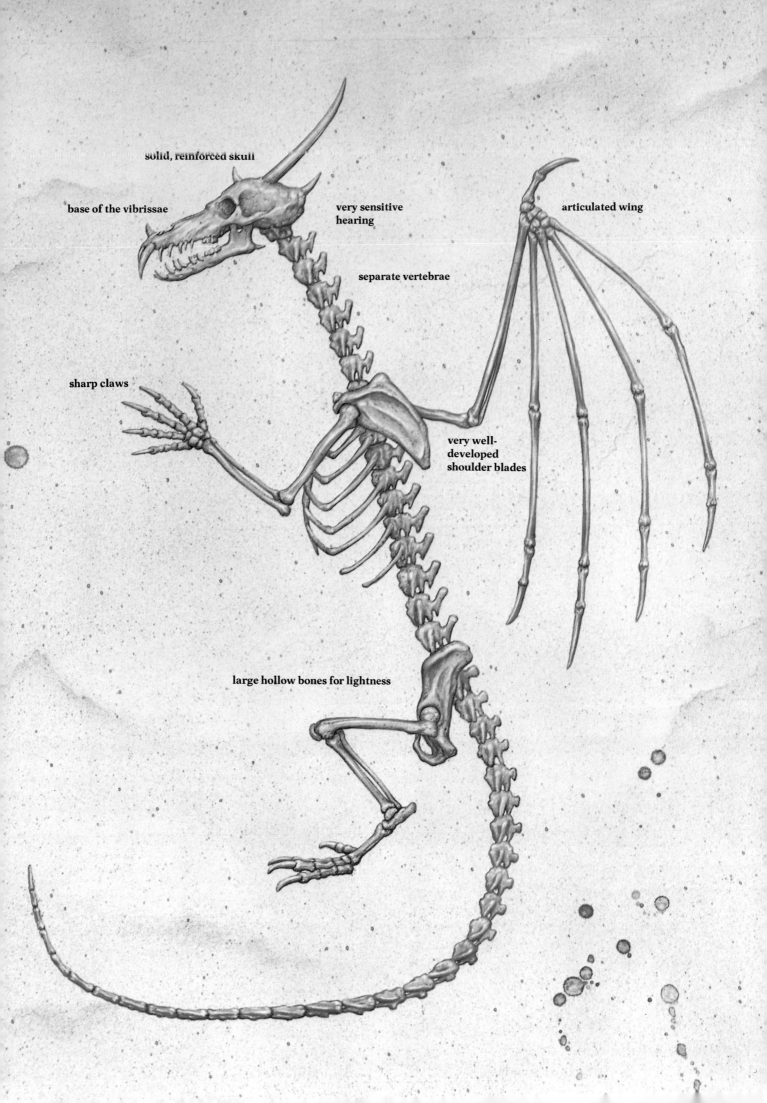

solid, reinforced skull

base of the vibrissae

very sensitive
hearing

articulated wing

separate vertebrae

sharp claws

very well-
developed
shoulder blades

large hollow bones for lightness

There are some dragons, experts in black magic, who are employed in the service of Evil. They use their powers to bewitch dragon servants who, even after the dragon's death, guard the dragon's abundant hoard of treasure. These terrible creatures practise black magic and are very difficult to thwart without the help of a very learned wizard.

The Scales

The dragon's body is completely covered with tough, shiny scales. The only exception is the Earth Dragon, or common dragon, who does not have this scaly armour on the neck or stomach, possibly due to his habit of burrowing underground. To protect his soft abdomen, this species often wears a jewelled breastplate. Using his saliva, which has powerful adhesive properties, and which he secretes on an empty stomach, the common dragon sticks precious stones on to his neck and stomach, for protection as well as adornment.

The scales are pentagonal, and shaped like a teardrop, with two long sides and two shorter ones, and a very short fifth side attached to the skin. The dragon can make them stand on end whenever he likes, to preen them. Remember, the dragon is a very clean creature and takes great care always to keep his skin and scales clean and immaculate.

In their normal position, the scales overlap very neatly and, thanks to a tiny cavity in the surface, they fit into each other to allow perfect freedom of movement.

If we study a scale closely, we observe the following characteristics: the innermost part is composed of a compact hairy formation firmly rooted in the epidermis. On the hair follicle there are some tiny glands which secrete a substance that adheres firmly to the skin.

This substance is rich in minerals, which determine the hardness and the colour of the dragon's scales. The external surface has a horny, translucent texture which gives the scales their habitual lustre.

CROSS SECTION

translucent horny surface

internal surface

hairy formation

coating of coloured minerals

The dragon does not need to slough off his skin like most other reptiles, as the scales grow and are renewed automatically, like human nails and hair. They are not shed from the body, except in cases of illness.

FRONTAL SECTION

translucent horny surface

hair-like roots

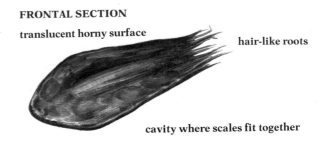

cavity where scales fit together

17

The mercenary warrior who hired himself out to towns and sovereigns to slay dragons usually wore a suit of armour made from dragon scales. This garment gave him enormous prestige and proclaimed to all and sundry that he had slain one of these fearsome beasts. Incidentally, the scales on his armour are very small, a clear indication that the dragon he killed was a young one who had barely reached puberty, and hence much easier to vanquish than an adult.

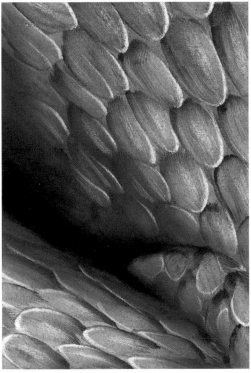

Colouring

It is impossible to list the enormous variety of hues that make up the dragon's brilliant colouring, but they can be divided into three broad colour groupings:

Blues, ranging from dark blue to silver and mother-of-pearl.
Reds, ranging from copper-red to dark red and reddish-black.
Greens, which include every imaginable shade of green and yellow and even dark brown, emerald green and burnished gold.

Although these three principle colour groups are not usually mixed, a dragon's colouring is rarely uniform. In general his scales are several hues from one of the main colour categories, with a metallic lustre which is hard to define. When the scales have a pale, opaque appearance it is a sure sign of ill health.

Many dragons are known by the predominant colour of their scales, such as Ancalagon the Black, Smaug the Golden and Spars the Green.

19

Dragons and Magic

The dragon is very well-versed in the art of magic, but not the dreaded black magic; he works with so-called brown or earth magic, green or plant magic and blue or water magic.

He knows how and to what extent he can manipulate nature for his own purposes without disturbing the ecological balance, for which he has always shown the utmost respect. He is able to invoke the power of the elements and can create illusions. He can invent disguises and maintain them for a long time, enabling him to escape his persecutors by appearing to be part of the landscape or by masquerading as a young child. There are countless legends in which human beings are transformed into monsters, evidence that originally they were young dragons who had not completely mastered their magic powers and were unable to maintain their illusory form.

Enormous powers of concentration are required to maintain a disguise for a long time and young dragons often lack the necessary application. Adult males, however, are able to preserve their chosen disguise for many days at a time, although they do need to rest at night, while the great dragon wizards are able to maintain an illusory form for months on end with only brief rest periods.

These dragon wizards hate the clumsy human wizards who, with no respect for the laws of nature, alter and often corrupt the life forces of the planet. The animosity is mutual. Human apprentices of magic envy the dragon his superiority in the occult sciences.

Indeed, the superior wisdom and tremendous power of the dragon aroused the hatred of medieval necromancers and priests, who taught people that dragons were the incarnation of evil and the devil. In medieval bestiaries, the figure of the dragon represented depravity and the diabolical, thus the dragon was often represented as a gargoyle.

A Captivating Voice

Music is one of the dragon's favourite pastimes, and he generally has a strong sense of rhythm. He also has a marvellous singing voice, and when he adopts a human guise, he is a virtuoso string instrumentalist. His voice, a rich bass or baritone, expresses great passion, arousing profound emotions in his audience. It is well-known that the sound of a dragon's voice has a bewitching effect on humans, and when he speaks, those reckless enough to pause and listen to him remain spellbound. Contrary to common belief, the dragon does not use this as a means of seducing his victims, but his beautiful, mellifluous voice and his impeccable diction are captivating, and anybody who speaks to the Dragon without taking precautions can fall under his spell and forget that they are in the presence of a terrible predator.

Although it is highly dangerous to talk to a dragon, he does not usually go in for surprise attacks or treachery, but even so, we are dealing with a depraved creature dedicated to the cause of Evil.

Dragons and Poetry

Dragons are passable poets and were probably the authors of many of the anonymous poems prior to the twelfth century that have survived until now through oral tradition. After conducting exhaustive investigations and rejecting dubious works of dragon troubadour poetry, we have managed to retrieve an example of dragon poetry:

> **VENI DULCIS AMICA MEA**
> **CUM QUA IOCARI ET SUAVIARI**
> **ET TENERAS DELICAS SUMERE**
> **ET IN AMORE FINIRE**

> *Come my sweet friend*
> *and play and kiss*
> *and enjoy those sweet delights*
> *and die in love.*

These lines come under the heading of courtly love poetry. This poem has come down to us signed by the knight Ambrosius de Jilocasin. He was the human form adopted by the earth dragon Jilocasin, the legendary adoptive father of two knights, who distinguished themselves during the reign of Charlemagne.

Although we do not know who wrote the following poem, its subject is reminiscent of the story of the dragon prince and one of Eleanor of Aquitaine's ladies. The poem vividly evokes the heartbroken lover's tragic farewell. The unhappy dragon prince could well have parted from his lover with these very words.

**DULCIS AMICA VALE, SINE TE
PROCUL HINC HABITATUS
ANXIUS ABSCEDO, QUI NON
CITO REDIAM
NON DISCEDO TAMEN TOTUS
REMANETQUI TECUM
COGITAMEN MEUM. DISCEDO
VIX EGO MECUM.**

*Farewell sweet friend, I must journey far
    from here without you,
I depart in sorrow for I shall not return
    for many a year
but I shall not be gone completely for
my thoughts remain with you.
With heavy heart I take my leave.*

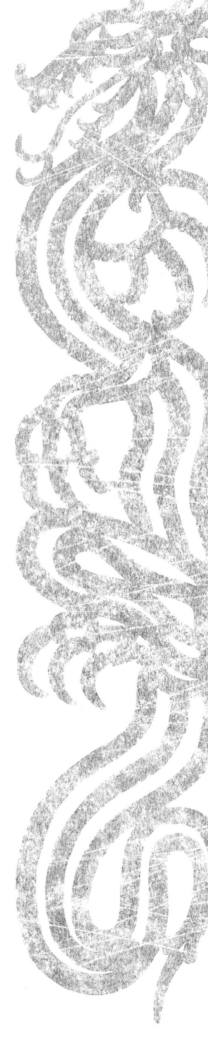

25

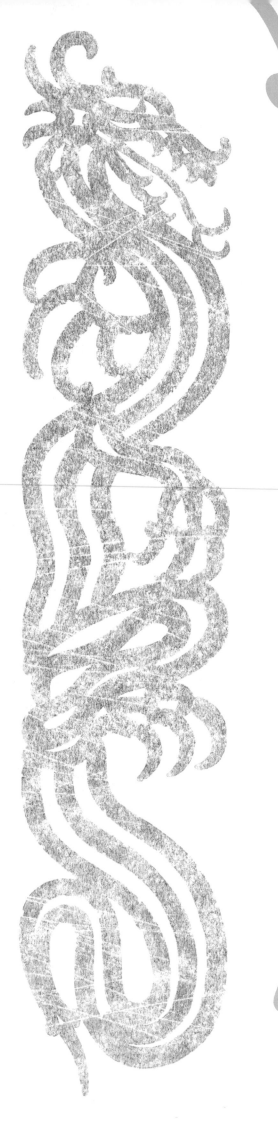

One of these, the mysterious Cercamon, was indisputably a dragon, and for a while he was a very close friend of the famous Marcabrú, the brilliant troubadour from Gascony. Cercamon's style, which was greatly influenced by his friend, is musical and gentle, as the following verse shows:

Quant l'aura doussa s'amarzis
e l fuelha chai de sul verjan
e l'auzelh chajan lor latis,
et ieu de sai sospir e chan
d'amour que.m te lassat e pres,
qu'ieu anc no l'agui en poder.

'When the gentle breeze becomes embittered
and the trees lose their foliage,
and the birds stop singing,
I too, sighing, sing of the love which
*   burns within me*
for it is not within my power to appease it.'

There is also evidence of a woman troubadour of unknown origin, who became famous for her happy verses and sweet songs. This was most unusual at a time when women poets gave their verses to minstrels to sing, and her life remains shrouded in mystery.

She was called the Comtessa de Día, and was in fact a young female dragon from the 'Draco splendens' family. She was so bold and conceited that she did not stop at writing poems – four of which have come down to us intact – she also became part of a band of wandering troubadours and even went so far as to make up her own life story.

He is young and happy
and I am young and happy,
my love is the handsomest,
for him I am beautiful and elegant;
since I am true to him,
he will always be true to me,
I will never betray his love,
and I know my love will never
    betray me.

Ab joi et ab joven m'apais
e iois e iovens m'apaia,
car mos amics es lo plus gais
per qu'ieu sui coindet'e gaia;
e pois eu li sui veraia
be.is taing q'el me sia verais,
c'anc de lui amar no m'estrais
ni ai cor que m'en estraia.

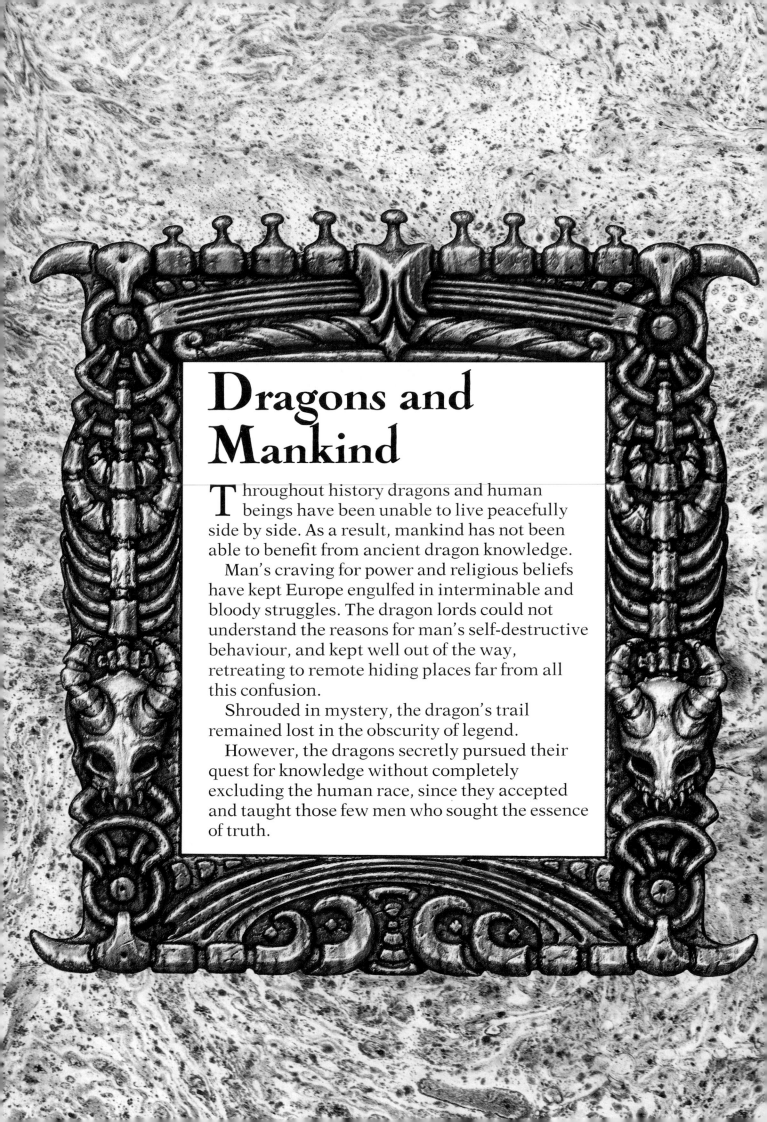

Dragons and Mankind

Throughout history dragons and human beings have been unable to live peacefully side by side. As a result, mankind has not been able to benefit from ancient dragon knowledge.

Man's craving for power and religious beliefs have kept Europe engulfed in interminable and bloody struggles. The dragon lords could not understand the reasons for man's self-destructive behaviour, and kept well out of the way, retreating to remote hiding places far from all this confusion.

Shrouded in mystery, the dragon's trail remained lost in the obscurity of legend.

However, the dragons secretly pursued their quest for knowledge without completely excluding the human race, since they accepted and taught those few men who sought the essence of truth.

Dragons and Riddles

Dragons are very fond of conundrums and riddles, and often try to outsmart each other. The dragons most renowned for their mental prowess take part in tournaments at the court of the Dragon Father.

Sometimes a free human being is admitted to these contests of wits, which we know about from one man who managed to beat his reptilian rivals in fair competition.

His name commands respect and admiration among both men and dragons, who confer on him the title Lord of the Dragon. This was the case of Merlin the magician, one of the few men

to win the affection of the dragon species
due to his prudent use of his great magic
powers and his consideration for nature.
He is the incarnation of wisdom and love
through the true nature of things.

This is the riddle he solved to win the
contest:

**IT IS COLD AND IT IS HOT
IT IS WHITE AND IT IS DARK
IT IS STONE AND IT IS WAX
BUT ITS TRUE NATURE IS MEAT
AND ITS COLOUR IS RED.**

The answer is: the human heart.

Art and Jewels

The dragon is a great lover of art, especially of gold and silver work, and he loves to hoard treasure. However, he is not renowned for his love of manual work, preferring intellectual activity by far. That is why he does not devote himself to creating jewels, but only to 'acquiring them' from human beings through various methods. Robbery, looting, trade, barter, fraud – by any means fair or foul which enables him to come by the jewels and precious stones he covets.

The dragon feels he never has enough jewels and he finds it difficult to part voluntarily with a single one of his treasures. Even though, for example, he gives jewels to the favourites in his family, he does it purely because he knows that the young maidens cannot remove the jewels to the outside world. He is very jealous of his belongings and guards the treasure he has built up over

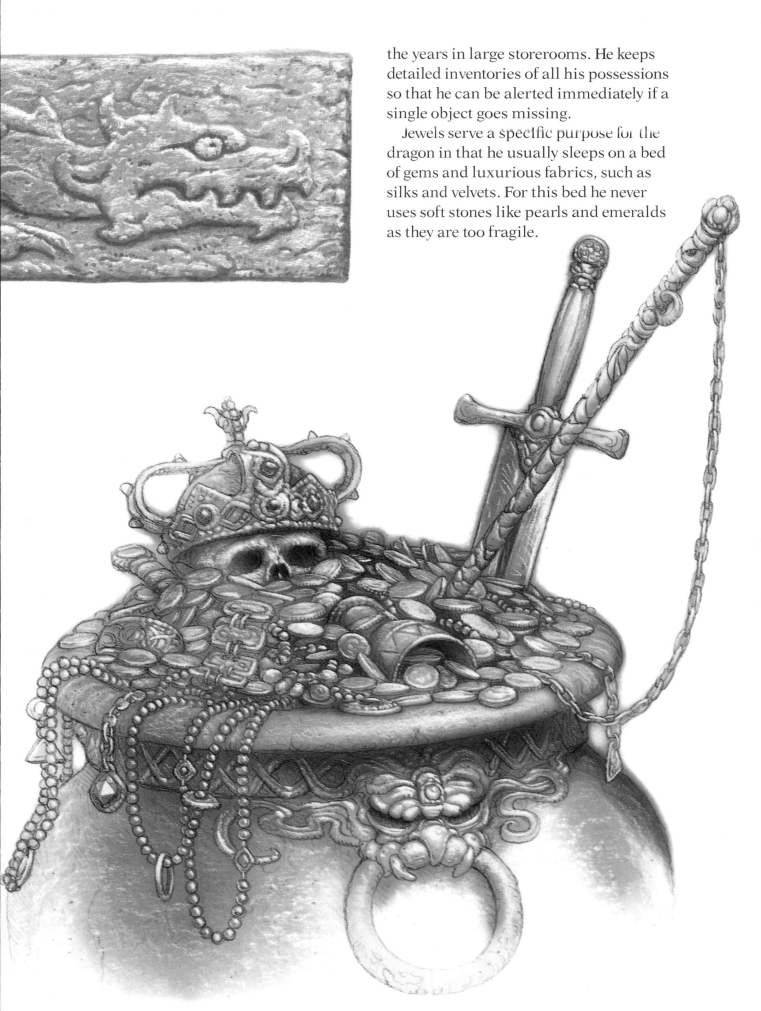

the years in large storerooms. He keeps detailed inventories of all his possessions so that he can be alerted immediately if a single object goes missing.

Jewels serve a specific purpose for the dragon in that he usually sleeps on a bed of gems and luxurious fabrics, such as silks and velvets. For this bed he never uses soft stones like pearls and emeralds as they are too fragile.

The Dragon's Abode

Dragons usually live in natural caves and caverns, which they adapt to their needs. The dragon's abode consists of two or more rooms, but the room closest to the entrance always retains its original aspect, to allay the suspicions of curious human beings. Normally, this entrance is concealed by plants and rocks and is just big enough to allow the creatures to go in and out. Over the years, the continual friction of the dragon's scaly body against the cave walls makes them smooth and polished. The dragon chooses a cave that is big enough for him to turn round in if he is pursued, but not so big that it can conceal an enemy.

The process of finding a home is always the same: the dragon emits an ultrasound vibration and the sensitive vibrissae or 'cats whiskers' around his mouth capture the echo, which enables him to locate the grottos in the vicinity.

He looks for two adjacent caves, and once he has identified the ones he wants, he digs a passage the exact width of his body to connect the two caves. He enlarges and polishes the inner cave with great care, checks that there are no chinks or ways out, and plugs any holes. Then he makes or gets his slaves to make a small ventilation hole.

As he requires more space, the dragon digs out new rooms, until he has created a cave complex where he can live comfortably with enough room for his slaves and treasures.

This is the most common type of dwelling among Earth Dragons and Water Dragons, but Fire Dragons have a different social structure and some very different habits and customs. In the chapters devoted to each different species we will give a more detailed description of these different types of abode, and the slaves and servants associated with each family.

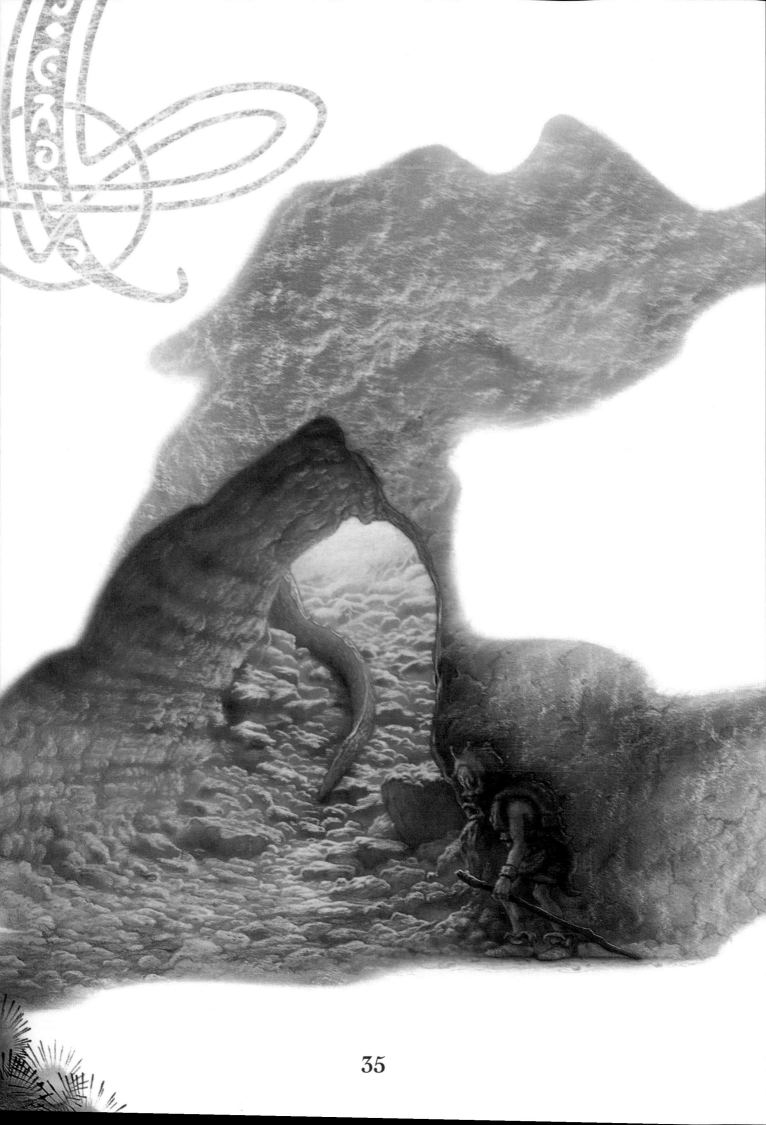

The Dragon Father

The various dragon families are organized into hierarchical societies revolving around the figure of a wise and judicious male, the head of the family, known as the Dragon Father. All the other dragons pledge obedience to him. It is his task to make peace and adjudicate when there are family quarrels or territorial disputes, which sometimes arise, and to confer a true name on each of his subjects.

This ancient male usually exercises his privileges with moderation. His court is made up of an unspecified number of young dragons who act as bodyguards and pages to the King, and young virgin female dragons who have not reached the required maturity to mate.

It is the Dragon Father who decides when the females are ready for mating. He is assisted by the elderly female dragons who are no longer fertile and have withdrawn, tired of wandering the world. These females, who are very well versed in magic, are given the title of Queen and hold full authority in the Regency Council. They select the candidates for the nuptial flight, and it is they who choose the successor to the Dragon Father on his death.

Female Dragons

Female dragons are very scarce, as we mentioned before, so they are treated with special care and attention. The male who incubates a female egg does not abandon the developing egg as is customary, but keeps a close watch on it, turning it over regularly.

When it is time for the egg to hatch, the anxious father takes it to a safe place, far from human settlements, and builds a nest well concealed from prying eyes. As soon as the baby female dragon emerges from the shell, he brings her food so that she can eat without venturing out of the nest. When the baby dragon is strong enough to hold on to her father's shoulders, he whisks her through the air to the dragon court, where she

will live with the rest of the young females until the Dragon Father considers her mature enough to mate.

As a result of being protected and raised by the group, the physical development of the young female is slower than that of the male, although she reaches maturity more rapidly. It is not unusual for the young female dragon to start talking before the wing sacs have disappeared.

Female dragons command great respect and are treated like queens. Often prouder and fiercer than males, they are very jealous of their privileges.

By the time the female dragon is ready for her first mating flight, she is generally a beautiful adult beast who has acquired the wisdom of the most learned wise woman, and received intensive instruction in all the fields of dragon knowledge. She sets out on this flight alone, but is joined by the males who wish to mate with her. She ends up at the centre of a swarm of several hundred fully developed male dragons.

The flight of dragons – which can easily be spotted due to its sheer size – travels towards the destination chosen by the Dragon Father for the union.

Young female dragons, who are expert magicians, sometimes change themselves into women of great beauty. As they are able to sustain this illusory personality for longer than the males, they have been known to enter human society without revealing their true identity, and to preserve their human form for a considerable length of time. Their memory lives on today in such legends as the enlightening story of Melusine.

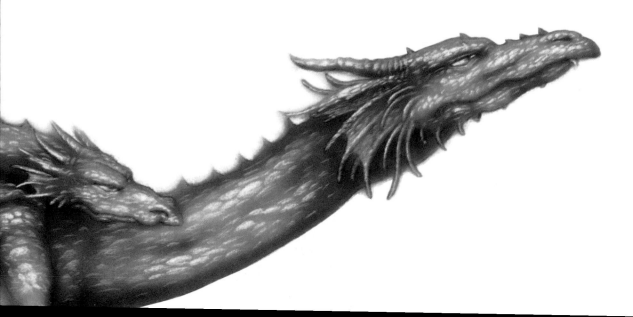

The Story of Melusine

This beautiful tale by Jean d'Arras narrates the events that took place in the castle of Lusignan, in the French region of Poitou.

One day, while out riding, the lord of Lusignan saw a beautiful woman who said her name was Melusine. He instantly fell passionately in love with the unknown woman and asked to marry her. Melusine consented on one condition: the knight should never try to look at her while she was bathing.

They lived happily for many years and had many children. Although she seemed totally human, the children born of their union possessed some strange traits, such as huge teeth and unusually brilliant eyes. When the lord of the castle of Lusignan, prompted by a jealous maiden, broke his word and spied on his wife in her bath, he discovered that Melusine changed into a dragon. The knight gave a howl of dismay and the dragon discovered her husband's betrayal. She fled forever from the castle.

From that moment misfortune dogged the Lusignan heirs. Local peasants say that each time a member of Melusine's family died, a dragon could be seen flying around the castle weeping copious tears.

Tradition also has it that in the Poitou region the dragon was sighted flying over the area, and weeping for the nobles who died during the French Revolution.

Favourites

The shortage of female dragons is another powerful influence on the social organization of the species and the dragon's capacity for forming emotional attachments.

The dragon mates only six or seven times in his lifetime if he is lucky. He can only stay with the female for a few hours, and this prevents him from becoming attached to his occasional mate.

However much the dragon, as an intelligent being, needs social and physical contact, he is unsociable by nature and profoundly competitive, seeing other dragons as potential rivals. This makes it impossible for him to form friendships with other dragons.

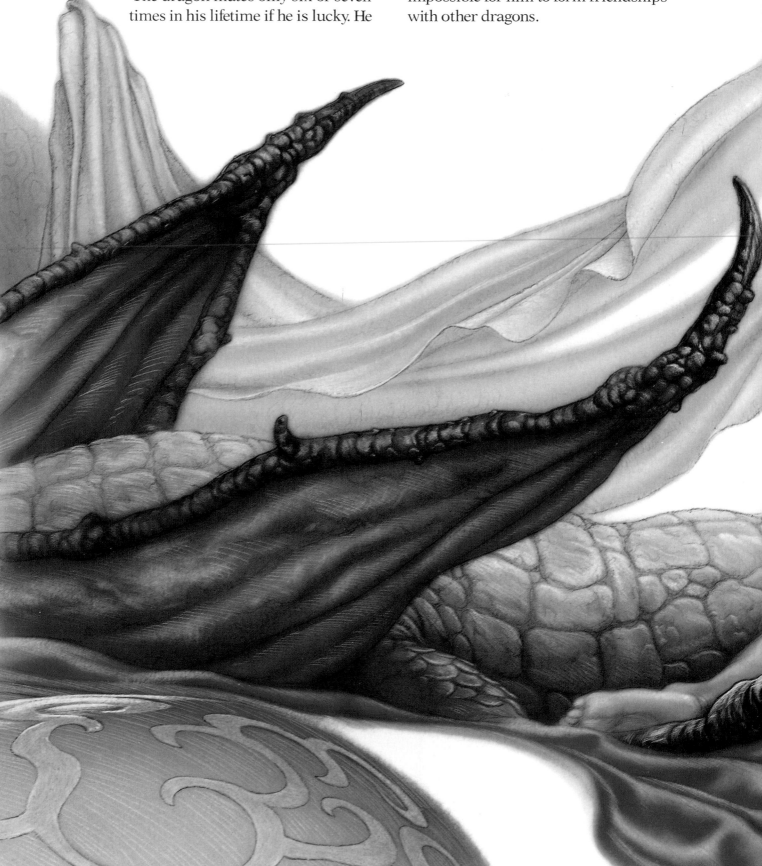

That frustration is why the dragon fulfils his need for affection with his 'favourites', usually human slaves kept almost as mascots. Pampered and spoilt by their master, the favourites usually sleep with the dragon, and their only obligation is to caress him, sing to him and accompany him whenever he wishes.

The dragon frequently chooses a new favourite, and when he does so, he usually releases the old one to avoid problems of jealousy.

These favourites should not be confused with the dragons' ladies. These are women with whom the dragon has forged a strong and lasting relationship. In this book there are two examples: the love of the Dragon Prince for the Lady of Aquitaine and that of Jilocasín for the Lady of Gascony.

The Dragon's Heritage

All dragons jealously guard in their homes some very ancient, shiny, round stones. Known as *Lapis draconiensis aurulucentis*, these stones have a natural phosphorescence. The dragon acquires them as part of his inheritance, or by looting, and they cannot be found anywhere else on earth. These stones are sacred for the dragon and he values them enormously, as they are a symbol of his identity.

There are a number of legends concerning these strange stones.

Even though they are closely guarded, there was a Norwegian dragon, several hundred years ago, from whom the gnomes stole the sacred stones after he was killed by a rival in a duel.

Despite their great strength, the dragons were never able to retrieve them, and this loss was a disaster for the species. Tradition has it that the stones come from a remote and wonderful planet known as the Shining Planet, where the 'great dragons' still live.

In the distant past, some members of the dragon species were expelled from this planet by the 'Father of All Dragons' as a punishment for trying to change nature to suit themselves, without

respecting the ecological balance and the life forces, and they were allowed to keep only these shiny stones as a reminder of their homeland and its glorious past.

This legend explains the dragons' respect for nature and the care they take not to disturb the ecological balance when practising magic.

They believe that if they observe the dragon code throughout their lives, they will be able to return to the Shining Planet to join the Great Dragon and be reunited with those who were not exiled.

Due to this belief, most dragons do not abuse their strength or power. But as they are intelligent beings with free will, there are some who stray from the code and take the path of darkness. These servants of Evil engage in battles, with the sole aim of spreading grief and destruction. Such is the case of one dragon who joined forces with the Lord of Darkness, and for centuries was the guardian of the infernal kingdoms, establishing a reign of terror and death.

It is interesting to note that the dragon code does not consider it an offence to steal from humans but gluttony is an unpardonable vice.

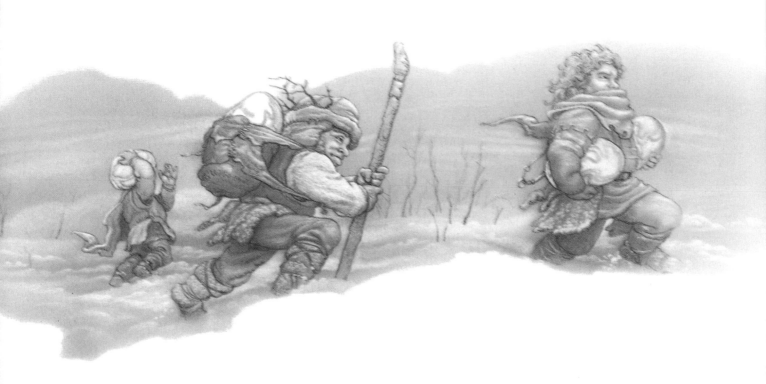

The Great Earth Dragon

The commonest and most abundant dragon species found on our planet is that of the Great Earth Dragon, or *Draco rex Cristatus*, as it is commonly called.

They are great winged creatures of enormous size. They can grow up to fifteen to thirty metres in length with a wing span of up to thirty metres. Their colouring is usually greeny-brown, with their many-hued scales ranging from lemon-yellow to emerald-green. There are some earth dragons who can breathe fire, although the force of their flames is not as powerful as that of the fire dragon.

The earth dragon is an expert flier and glider. Although his great size sometimes makes take-off awkward, once in the air he can reach great altitudes and cover enormous distances by gliding, using solely the wind.

The *Draco rex* is reserved by nature and an introvert. He does not like being around members of his species other than in the mating season and even then only for a limited time. This behaviour seems to be governed by the wish to avoid disputes over food and the possession of the female. Given the size and strength of dragons, such squabbles could be dangerous. Interestingly though, when an earth dragon grows old, it is not unusual for him to be accompanied by a young page, whom he will instruct in dragon wisdom and who will inherit all his wealth.

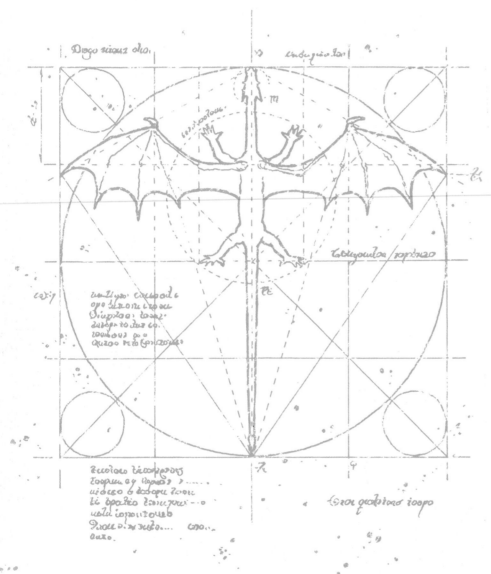

The Egg

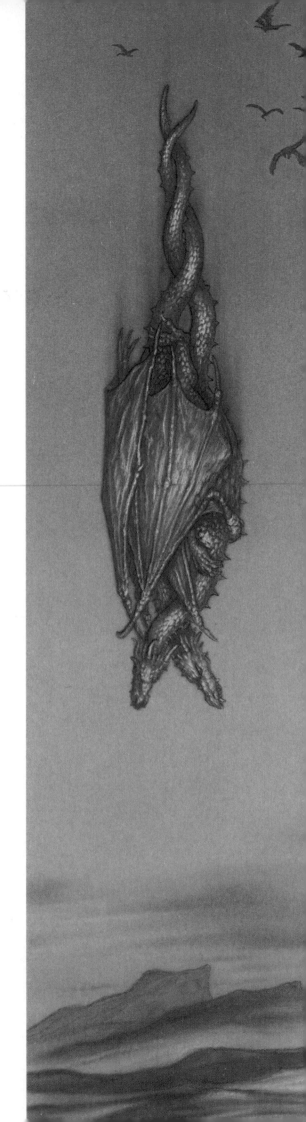

Earth dragons mate only during very rainy seasons, when the African and Asian deserts are carpeted with flowers. On these occasions, the males congregate around a female who sets off on her nuptial flight. Although the females are always bigger than the males, they are extremely agile in the air. When a female soars up into the air the males pursue her in a ballet of graceful, aerial acrobatics.

The most agile dragon eventually catches up with her. He waits for the moment when the female unfolds her wings to their maximum span and then their union takes place at a great height. He slides under the belly of his beloved and enfolds her in an embrace of wings and talons. Thus entwined, the pair reach their climax while plunging rapidly down to earth. Only when they are a few metres from the ground do they part and spread their wings to land.

After the nuptial flight, the couple withdraw to the heart of the desert, and there the female makes a nest in the warm, damp sand where she lays a single egg, about the size of an ostrich egg, and curiously mottled green and grey.

The female abandons the egg, leaving the father to look after it. He keeps the egg warm to stimulate the hardening of

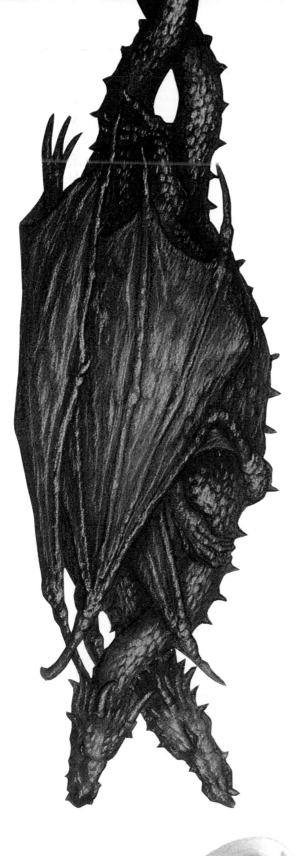

the shell. Meanwhile, the female returns to the place where the other males are waiting for her and the mating ritual begins all over again. The nuptial flight is repeated as many times as is necessary until all the males have an egg. However, from all these unions only one female will be born, for only the dragon's first egg contains a female embryo. As the days go by, the humidity of the sand changes, and the last eggs have little chance of hardening sufficiently to hatch. Thus the law of natural selection prevails and the only dragons who reproduce are the ones who manage to mate with the female during the early flights.

When the egg has hardened sufficiently and is ready to hatch, the doting father takes it to a suitable place for the young dragon, usually in the temperate Mediterranean forests, where it will be easy to find food. In general, he places the egg in a hole or in a small cave out of reach of predators, and blocks the entrance leaving only a small opening.

The dragon abandons his young the minute he has found a safe place, and he never hunts in the nearby area, so as not to give away the hiding place. However, he continues to keep watch over the area, flying backwards and forwards at great height to avoid being seen.

The Young

Baby earth dragons might easily be mistaken for large lizards, like the eyed lizard, which is very common in some parts of Europe.

Newly hatched dragons measure some sixty centimetres in length, and their wings, encased in sacs, look at first glance like typical lizard markings.

The baby dragon's tail is not ring-shaped, and if caught, he is not able to shed it like other reptiles. Thanks to his relatively large size and his tremendous

agility, he is able to elude predators such as foxes, badgers and birds of prey which would otherwise devour him.

At about eight or nine months, he is the size of a large dog, and is now able to tackle animals as large and fierce as a wolf. He hunts and eats foxes and mountain goats, as well as stray sheep and calves, but always with moderation to avoid discovery by humans. This behaviour is instinctive in the young dragon, whose intelligence has not yet developed. His nocturnal habits, his caution and his extreme timidity make it

very difficult to observe the young dragon during this period. When he enters adolescence, at around the age of two, the father ceases his vigilance and gradually the young dragon is left to his own devices.

The adolescent dragon has already attained a considerable size, which makes camouflage difficult. At about this time, his wings may begin to unfold, and his intelligence becomes more acute as the proverbial cunning of the species starts to manifest itself. As his innate knowledge of Latin develops, he learns

the idiom of the region where he lives and begins to hunt, devouring everything he comes across, from flocks of sheep to men and women.

In these early years, the adolescent dragon is usually a proud fighter, with little inclination towards poetry and magic, and that is when he can wreak the greatest havoc.

He has no fixed abode yet and he is not in the service of another dragon, but he has already developed a love of jewels and started to collect precious stones, which he uses as a bed and as a breastplate for his soft belly. He already feels the urge to accumulate wealth.

When he reaches the age of four, the young dragon flies to the court of the Dragon Father, where he will live for a couple of years to learn dragon social customs and be initiated into the art of magic. When this period is over he receives his secret name, and now the dragon is ready to settle down, either independently, or as a page to an adult male who will take him under his wing. During this period, he is not ready to reproduce.

Social Organization

As we enter the spacious cave complex which is the earth dragon's abode, we first come across a crudely excavated entrance cave, with a narrow corridor with very highly polished walls leading to the inner cave. The bedroom, where the treasure which serves as his bed is carefully arranged, is usually the central cave. This room, considered as the royal apartment, is always kept clean and tidy and is often adorned with beautiful and rare objects, tastefully arranged by the servants. These include luminous mosses and strangely shaped roots and stones, sculptures and artefacts of gold and silverwork – the spoils from the dragon's looting. Behind this room are the slaves' quarters as well as a cave, which is much smaller than the royal apartment where the dragon's page sleeps.

The common belief that dragons are dirty and unkempt, and that their homes are full of food leftovers is groundless. Like all animals that live in caves and burrows, they like to keep their home clean and tidy. It is the slaves' job to carry out these domestic duties.

The earth dragon's slaves are gnomes, elves and other woodland creatures, and above all human beings. Some are captured by the dragon himself, and others are acquired through exchanges with other dragons. The servants' duties include cleaning and arranging the home, as well as brushing and cleaning their master's scales and keeping him company. They do not lead a wretched life, as might be expected, for their masters

are not generally cruel to them, but treat them with kindness and generosity. The notion that dragons eat their servants when they are old and have outlived their usefulness is completely false. In fact this only happened on two occasions.

In both cases the dragons in question were very old and suffering from 'senile dementia', a brain-wasting disease which affects the members of this dragon family due to the enormous quantity of meat and fat they consume.

More usually a friendship develops between the dragon and his slaves, and often the servants accompany their masters to the celebrations held every five years at the court of the Dragon Father. Remember, the dragon does not build up relationships with other members of his species very easily.

The dragon shows a preference for pretty young slaves with good singing voices, for the dragons' love of music is legendary.

A human slave with these attributes can become the dragon's favourite, and he will sleep with his head in her soft

lap, and adorn her with jewels when he presents her at the court of the Dragon Father, who is very tolerant towards his subjects' whims. Much has been written about dragons who have offered friendship to their servants or to free human beings. There are even instances of a profound and genuine affection between a dragon and a human being.

Such is the story of Crisofilax, a dragon who signed a pact of friendship with King Egidius, and who lived for years in the capital of the tiny state.

Similarly, the *Crónicas de los Nuevos Reinos* (*Chronicles of the New Kingdoms*) tell of the case of Jilocasín, a dragon who, on losing his own young, adopted the first-born son of a lady. He brought the boy up and educated him like his own son, born of this same lady, and he succeeded in making both of them armed knights. The wise and judicious Jilocasín died defending his offspring against a female dragon who was jealous of the fame of the two young men, known as the Knights of the Dragon.

Water Dragons

The water dragon, or *Draco Splendens*, is rarer than the common dragon. He can be found in both salt and fresh water, although he prefers lakes.

Magnificently coloured, this beast is perfectly at home in water, moving through it with great agility and speed. Although his front legs end in sharp claws, his back legs have been transformed into fins, which hamper his movements on land.

He has a tremendous lung capacity and can store oxygen in his stomach and transfer it to the lungs when he needs it, which enables him to remain underwater for hours on end. Because he lives in water, this dragon has partially lost the ability to fly, and makes only short gliding flights, although some of them can attain a reasonable air speed.

Water dragons have very specific eating habits, especially the adults, which is why the few remaining examples are in danger of extinction.

Apparently, the water dragon only eats virgins. If this requirement is not satisfied, as is often the case, legend has it that the animal suffers excruciating indigestion which leaves him at death's door. The only cure considered effective consists of massive doses of virgin olive oil and a concoction made from orange blossom and magnolia petals.

The water dragon is physically much more beautiful and graceful than the earth dragon. He has a soft, tuneful voice and cherishes beauty above all else. He is an inspired poet and can spend hours contemplating his own reflection in the water, in a narcissistic pose, or go into ecstasies over a beautiful sunset. There are stories of dragons who have rejected the maiden they were about to eat because she was not beautiful, or not correctly attired, for they like their victim to be dressed in sumptuous silks with a circlet of fresh flowers in her hair.

The water dragon is also an amorous creature, and there have been occasions when the maiden destined for his dinner has become the queen of his heart.

He is a brave adversary and if called upon to fight will defend himself ferociously and to the death. However, he is shy, and it is not possible to catch more than a glimpse of him. He always conducts himself with elegance, even when capturing food.

The behaviour of the *Draco Splendens* is very different from *Draco rex cristatus*.

One curious fact is that this delicate and beautiful creature cannot bear any kind of chains or bonds around his neck, for this is the method that was used in antiquity to capture him. It was sufficient to tie a noose around his neck and the dragon would allow himself to be led away without a struggle. That is how dragons such as St George's dragon, the dragon of Sant Mer de Banyoles and the dragons of Santa Margarita and of Llac Negre were captured.

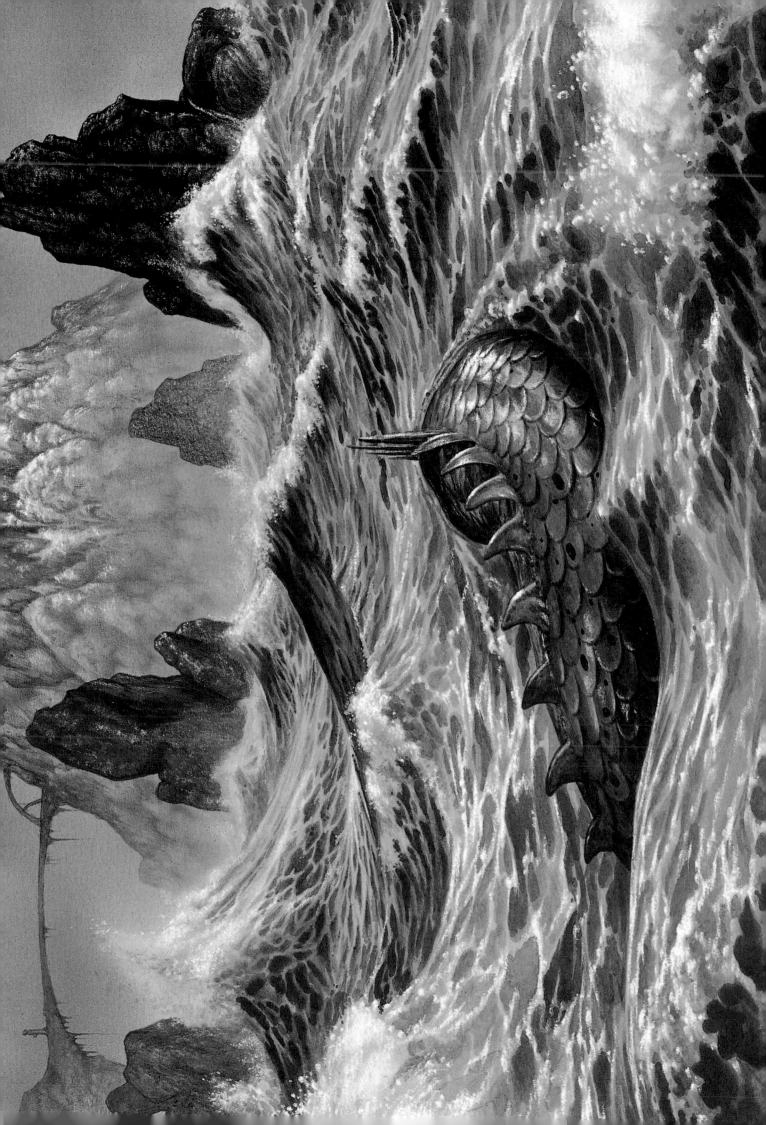

Dragons as Sea Serpents

Throughout history, water dragons have often been sighted, with the most recent incidents dating back to the beginning of the twentieth century.

The most scientifically reliable description is that of Peter Karl van Esling, the director of The Hague Zoo, who gives an account of a water dragon sighted during a voyage to collect marine species in the Atlantic in 1860:

'We saw a gigantic reptile, bright blue and silver in colour. He swam gracefully around the ship before the sailors' eyes, and submerged himself without a splash. His eyes were enormous, with vertical pupils and an intelligent expression. They seemed luminous, but this effect could be due to the reflections from the setting sun.

'His head was adorned with bright blue and green crests. Even though he disappeared under water and we did not see him again, he appeared to measure some seven metres in length, and on his back we could make out something resembling crests or fins. I think he was serpent-like, but the sailor beside me thought he saw legs and claws.

'We baptized him Megophias.'

Mating and the Young

We know about the life cycle of *Draco splendens* thanks to the investigations of the eminent English botanist and explorer, Sir Reginald Wort, who at the close of the eighteenth century spent months observing the fauna of the Zaragoza sea.

In the course of his investigations into water dragons, the British aristocrat witnessed the nuptial ceremonies of this species. His patient observations have given us the following account:

'The female on heat looks for a seaweed-covered bed on which she lies and emits a luminescent glow. Her brilliant colours cause the males to launch into an energetic display of acrobatics. They leap into the air only to disappear again, resembling streaks of light.

'The female being courted then swims rapidly down to the depths of the ocean, followed by the throng of males. Only the fastest and strongest succeed in mating with her. After coupling has taken place, the female dragon hands over the fertilized egg to her partner, who deposits it in the warm sands of a safe beach and watches over it until it hatches. When the young dragon hatches, the father's duty is done, and he disappears, partly so as not to betray the

young dragon's presence to predators. During his lonely infancy, the young dragon feeds on tropical fruits and is strictly vegetarian.'

However Sir Reginald was wrong on one point. The little dragon is not abandoned as would appear from casual observation. The father visits his young at night, and during the day he keeps watch over the area from a prudent distance. The truth of this is borne out by the dramatic fate which befell a bold but inexperienced naturalist as told in the *Diary of Expeditions and Discoveries of the New World* by the Portuguese adventurer, Da Silva, in 1612:

'Paulo and the young André Do Gao disembarked on the lush island, which seemed to be inhabited only by birds and crabs. Paulo saw a huge brilliantly coloured water lizard which appeared to be quite tame but very timid. He called his companion and they managed to catch the animal.

'When the two naturalists wanted to bring him on board, the animal let out a series of shrill howls and from the sea appeared an enormous lizard which threw itself on the unfortunate pair. André died in the fray, with his head virtually torn from his body, and Paulo managed to survive because he threw the basket with the young lizard into the sea. Immediately, the sea monster abandoned the pursuit to save the drowning animal.

'We were so overwhelmed by this incident that we did not dare return to the island to recover André's body and bury him.'

This little-known tale was considered spurious in scientific circles at the time, but it confirms our observations on the behaviour of *Draco splendens*.

The Development of Draco Splendens

When a young *Draco splendens* has grown to one metre, his colouring becomes brighter and more luminous. He loves the water and soon learns to swim. When the father believes the young dragon is able to swim, he abandons him once and for all and continues his adult life elsewhere. During his first days alone, the young dragon often howls pitifully, but he soon gets used to it. His instinct prompts him to take to the water, leaving the land for ever. During this phase he feeds solely on sea anemones, which do not harm him even though they are poisonous.

Draco splendens' first destination is the underwater cave where the Dragon Father's court resides. There he grows up and receives his education, and after a while every young dragon follows the Gulf Stream and sets off in search of a place to make his permanent home.

During this journey, he reaches full maturity. By the time he reaches the European shores, he is a magnificent animal measuring seven metres in length, brilliantly coloured and beautiful to behold. He has mastered the power of speech and is an expert magician. Carried by subterranean currents unknown to man, he penetrates the European mainland. He cannot tolerate polluted water and eats only once a month, feasting as usual on virgins.

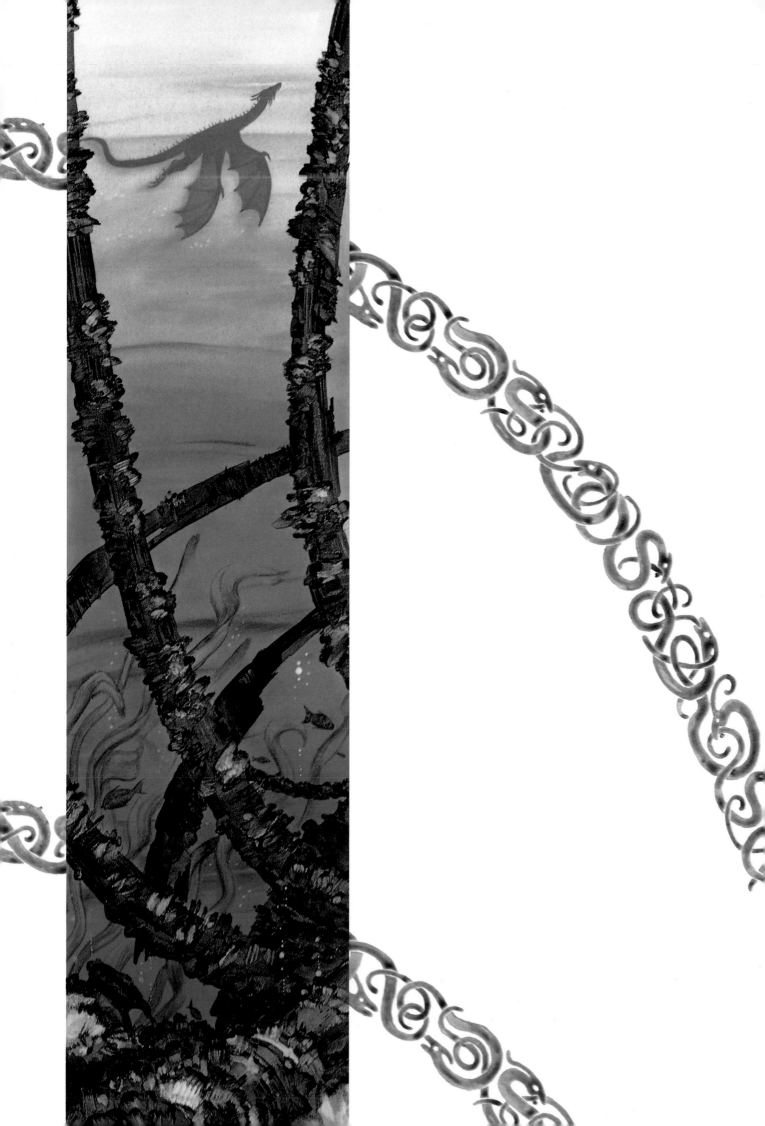

The Water Dragon's Abode

The usual home of *Draco splendens* is a cave with a submerged entrance. Curiously, this cave is always dry and the floor is covered with sand that the dragon himself brings from the beach. This complex of caves is bigger and more elaborately fashioned than that of the common dragon. The rooms are decorated with pearls, corals and gems of great beauty, which the owner has collected over the years, and with which he creates original and elaborate patterns. Stalactites and stalagmites are also part of the cave's decor while artistically arranged vases of flowers enhance the rooms.

It is not unusual for one of the caves to have a subterranean stream running through it. The dragon swims in it and his slaves drink the water and bathe in it.

The water dragon's family is small but select. It is usually made up of water creatures such as lower class water sprites, with little magic power, small newts and a few human beings. He never captures water nymphs or sprites from the large rivers, for they are very powerful.

Among the human beings are poets and troubadours, and, very often, the maiden of his dreams.

The dragon's lady is both his mistress and his slave, and he lives surrounded by a select entourage of damsels, pages and squires. When the dragon keeps humans in his cave he usually makes a small opening so that they can leave easily. His taste for art and his exclusive feeding habits mean that this dragon family has frequent contact with humans.

The Fire Dragon

The rarest of the three species is *Draco flameus*. It is extremely difficult to observe and study this dragon, since his habitat is inaccessible to human beings. This virtually unknown dragon lives inside active volcanoes, and his natural surroundings are the great rivers of lava and the fiery caverns in the belly of the earth.

In this world of fire and incandescent molten rock dwells the Dragon Father, and this is where courtship and mating take place, rituals which no human being has ever witnessed. The fire dragon spends his infancy in these suffocating surroundings, and only when he reaches maturity does he venture outside on brief hunting expeditions.

A nocturnal creature, he usually sallies forth enveloped in flames, when darkness reigns, but only if the weather is very dry and the sky clear. Water and humidity are a great threat to these creatures since they can cause 'scale corrosion', a fatal disease for *Draco flameus*.

On his excursions into the outside world, the fire dragon sets vast expanses of land aflame, scorching everything in his path, and then avidly devours the charred remains of the animals left in the ashes. He breathes fire from his mouth due to a mixture of phosphorous and methane which he produces and stores in a second stomach. The mixture ignites on contact with oxygen as it leaves the dragon's mouth.

His favourite food is hydrocarbons, such as oil and bitumen, which he consumes in huge quantities. He also uses these substances to clean and shine his 'armour' - an occupation to which the fire dragon devotes many hours. He takes great care of every single scale and is always on the lookout for any suspicious-looking blemishes. This is not a question of vanity, even though the dragon is a very conceited creature, but because he needs to guard against his most deadly enemy, 'scale corrosion', as mentioned earlier.

This terrible disease causes the scales to flake off from the body, leaving the dragon's sensitive skin exposed and vulnerable, not only to the dreadful burns produced by red-hot lava but also to total dehydration, as a result of the intense heat of his surroundings.

The scales, which cover his entire body, are made up of a metal and asbestos alloy. They are many-coloured, ranging from bright golden-yellows to red, copper and black, and these scales are the dragon's only protection against fire. Without this armour, he is as susceptible to heat as any other living creature.

Apparently this species used to be abundant in the volcanoes of Iceland, and he would fly as far as Ireland and the north of Britain. It is also said that a small colony of this species has survived in Sicily. On the other hand, there is no evidence of the existence of fire dragons in Vesuvius.

This mysterious but fascinating animal has a large family of servants made up mainly of salamanders, will-o'the-wisps and other igneous creatures.

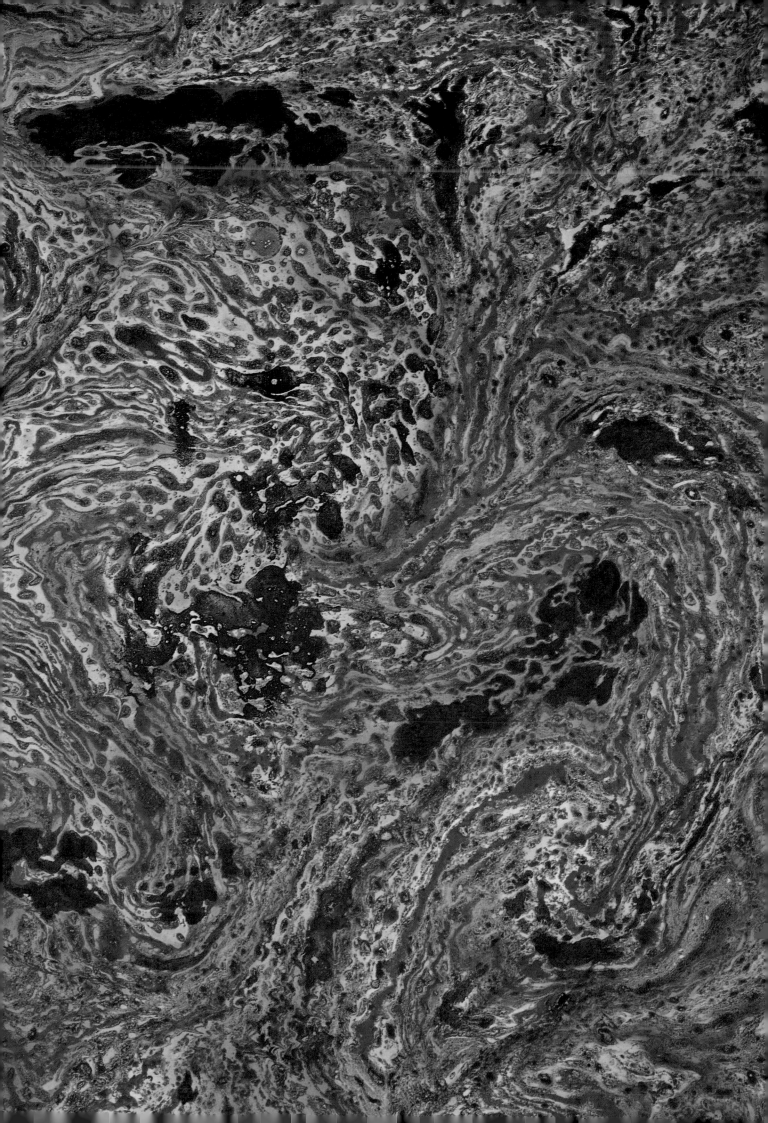

Social Organization of the Fire Dragon

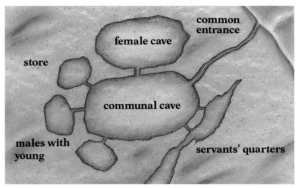

As we said earlier, the fire dragon lives in a vast complex of caves inside craters, among streams of lava and suffocating gases. Despite his strange and fearsome habitat, this is the most amicable and peace-loving of the great dragon races, and also the most gregarious and outgoing. Fire dragon society is organized into three large matriarchal groups. A powerful and sexually mature female occupies the principle cave of a colony formed by the males and their sons. As is usual with dragons, only paternity is recognized, and the young are not considered descendants of the female, but offspring of the male. Consequently, a female dragon does not object to a male joining her colony with an egg from another female.

Despite this matriarchal structure, the great dragon family continues to be governed by a Dragon Father, but in this case the hierarchy is not so rigid. And given that the habitat of the fire dragon is restricted and the colonies are very close to each other and linked by narrow corridors, animals of the same age and sex live together, play together and learn together. This cohabitation with other members of the same species means that the fire dragon has the least contact with human beings, given that they can satisfy their emotional needs among their own kind, either in couples or through friendship with their neighbours in the colony. They usually practise many group activities, although they always hunt alone so as not to frighten off the prey.

The Little Fire Dragon

The *Draco flamula*, which is usually under two metres in length, is a sub-species of the fire dragon. He lives in the chimneys of power stations, and has adapted perfectly to the high

temperatures and the concentrations of sulphur and sulphuric acid. His scales have also taken on the sulphur-yellow and rust tones that facilitate his camouflage and make it almost impossible to distinguish him.

The first human being to see and identify this species was an engineer in a Bavarian power station who was a dragon fan. He gave it the name of *flamula*, because of the little tongue of flickering flame the dragon produces when he emerges from the chimney.

This sub-species is powerful and destructive because when these creatures fly they leave a trail of sulphurous gases that produce acid rain, a phenomenon which destroys trees and has damaged vast areas of woodland in Great Britain, Germany and Spain. Scholars believe that these animals are a throwback of the dragon race rather than an evolution of the species adapted to new surroundings. This theory seems to be borne out by the loss of Latin as their principal language (they are not known to speak any other language either) and by the absence of a stable social organization. Apparently the other species of dragons despise and loathe these diminutive relatives.

The Sicilian Dragon

Another sub-species of the fire dragon is *Estupidus catalanus*, which is very rare and found only in the craters of Mount Etna, in Sicily. Local inhabitants claim that it was brought over by the Catalan conquistadors of the Middle Ages.

This animal, with its lustreless colours and short legs, was described at the beginning of the century by Professor Peter Ameisenhaufen, who baptised him *Pirofagus estupidus catalanus* due to his presumed origin, which is actually highly dubious, as far as we can see. He breathes fire like all the fire dragons, but on inhaling he breathes in the flames and this causes painful burns in the oesophagus. He has to drink enormous quantities of water to soothe them. He lacks the dragon's traditional faculty of speech, and the evidence seems to point to a very limited intelligence. In his work *Fauna secreta*, Professor Ameisenhaufen branded this unendearing creature an 'accident of evolution'.

The Golden Dragon

Most revered among the dragons' legendary heroes is the golden dragon. His scales and wings are the colour of gold, and, although he does not belong to any of the three great elements (earth, water and fire), by nature he embraces all three, and he is the dragon possessed of the greatest beauty. He is unique, pure and perfect. Neither fire, nor air nor water are strangers to him. Only one man is his friend and only three knights have ever set eyes on him.

To become acquainted with this strange being we must consult the *Book of the Golden Dragon*, one of the sacred books of dragon culture.

'The Golden Dragon has never taken part in any aggressive action. Unsullied by any flaw, he is pure and without blemish. He is the Guardian.

'He defends the Enchanted Castle where a pure-hearted knight devotedly guards the Sacred Chalice.

'The Sacred Chalice is the font of peace, nature and life. It was concealed from the eyes of humans because they

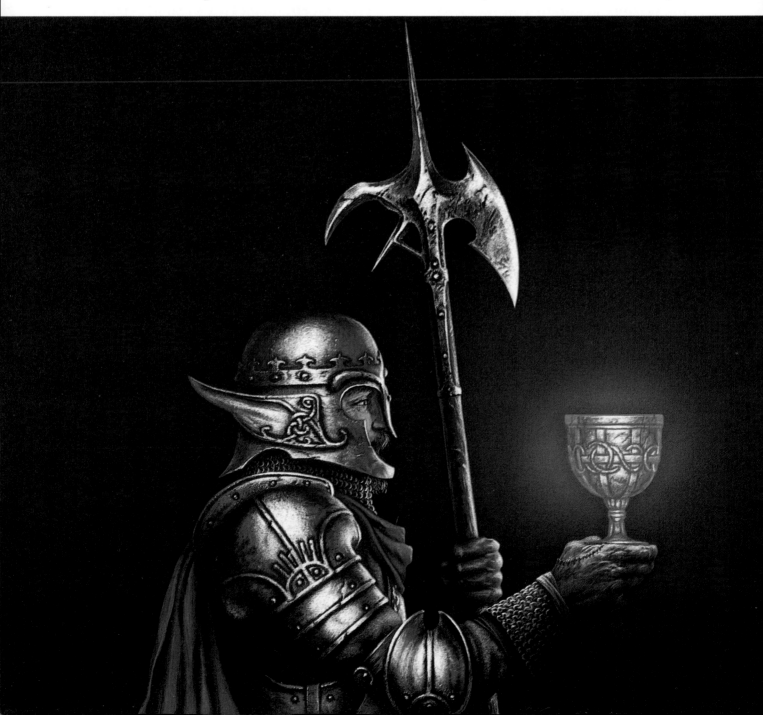

were not worthy of it. Only three knights succeeded in attaining it, and only one, who was free from sin, became its King. Before the astonished gaze of his two companions, the pure-hearted knight and the Sacred Chalice were plucked from Earth with the promise that they would be returned when the dwellers of this world were worthy of beholding the chalice and drinking from it.

'The Golden Dragon was summoned to carry the Guardian knight to the Enchanted Castle, in the heart of the Hidden Wood, and to watch over him until the Sacred Chalice returns to Earth. Then, all the Dragons will fly to meet him, carrying on their backs pure men, and all will pay homage to the Bearer of the Chalice and to the Golden Dragon. And then all Nature will be cured of its wounds. Fear and hatred will disappear. Virgins and dragons will be friends, and the era of Peace will dawn, shrouded in the golden radiance of the Sacred Chalice and in the sweetness of its life-giving Light.'

This myth has much in common with the legend of the Holy Grail and of Sir Galahad, which could indicate that dragons and poets were cast in the same mould, or that the Holy Grail and the knights really did exist.

The Golden Apples

The most powerful of all the Greek heroes was Heracles, the son of Zeus and Alcmene. Eurystheus, the king of Mycenae and Tiryns was very jealous of him, and set him Twelve Labours, including one almost impossible task: Heracles was to bring back the golden apples which were hidden in a divine garden and guarded by the terrible dragon Ladon and the daughters of the night, known as the Hesperides. The problem was that nobody knew where this garden was.

Heracles obediently set out to find the mysterious place, for he was eager to perform great feats. He searched, he questioned and he enquired, but to no avail.

Finally, Nereus, the sea god, told him what he wanted to know: the Garden of the Hesperides lay in an enchanted place beyond the edge of the world, where the Titan Atlas supported the vault of Heaven on his powerful shoulders.

The demigod set off immediately. He journeyed through unknown places full of danger, confronting monstrous and bloodthirsty creatures, and at last arrived at the place where Atlas held up the sky on his shoulders. Nearby lay the beautiful garden surrounded by fragrant honeysuckle and rambling roses. The air echoed with the bubbling laughter of the beautiful nymphs who were playing with the dragon, chasing each other through the trees.

The son of Zeus, dressed only in a lion's pelt and wielding an enormous club, was afraid that the Hesperides would be frightened of his appearance and his powerful weapon and did not dare enter. He went over to the giant and said: 'Powerful Atlas, you know the nymphs. Couldn't you go into the garden and pick the apples? They won't be afraid of you. Meanwhile I'll hold up the

sky for you'.

Atlas gladly agreed and hastily placed the celestial vault on to the shoulders of the demigod. Then, with a happy smile and a wave, he entered the garden.

From where he was standing, Hericles could hear the shrieks of surprise and joy of the young women at the sight of the titan, and the deeper voice of the dragon, welcoming him. For three days he heard nothing more of Atlas than the ringing of laughter and games in the divine garden. On the third day, Atlas appeared with the apples, which he placed at the hero's feet.

'Heracles my friend,' he said, 'I have spoken with the dragon, who is very intelligent, and he told me that the Hesperides are furious at losing the apples, and besides, I'm tired of holding up the sky without ever being able to

have any fun. I tell you, I had a lovely time with the dragon and the nymphs,' he added with a wink. 'I'm leaving you here, my friend, to hold up the sky, and I'm going to go and live in the divine garden. But to show you that I have kept my word, I have brought you the apples. Don't hold it against me.'

'That is good, I understand,' Heracles assured him, 'if I were you I would do exactly the same. Let me ask you just one favour.'

'Ask me whatever you like.'

'You may be able to hold up the celestial vault without effort, but I am not so accustomed to it and it's slipping. I'd like to put a rope cushion on my head to stop it from falling.'

'That seems fair to me,' replied the giant, 'I will hold it for you while you put the cushion on your head.' And the guileless giant took the sky so that Heracles could arrange the protective cushion on his head. The demigod, who was waiting for just that, ducked out of the way as fast as he could, picked up the apples and fled.

'Dragon, dragon, he's escaping!' shouted the furious Atlas but the dragon poked his head out of the garden gate and replied:

'You are so stupid that you deserve your fate. I warned you not to trust the hero. Now nobody can take your place.' And, as the Hesperides were calling him to play hide and seek, he went back into the garden leaving poor Atlas alone and bored with his burden.

The Ethiopian Dragon

Long ago, Ethiopia was ruled by King Cepheus and Queen Cassiopeia, who boasted that she was more beautiful than all the Nereids. Furious at this insult, the daughters of the sea complained to the god Poseidon, asking him to avenge them. He sent a dragon, who devastated the land and devoured the young people of Ethiopia. The terrified population consulted the oracle Ammon, who told them that their only hope of deliverance would be to hand over to the dragon the beautiful Andromeda, daughter of the King and Queen. Cepheus and Cassiopeia were reluctant to surrender their daughter, but pressured by their subjects, they finally agreed to the sacrifice. The soldiers chained the maiden to a rock in the middle of the sea where the monster lived.

Weeping and lamenting, the princess's parents waited on the shore. It just so happened that the young Perseus, the son of Zeus, was passing that way on his winged horse Pegasus. On seeing the desperate sovereigns, the hero, who had just killed the terrible Medusa, stopped to ask them what was wrong. Sobbing, the King and Queen told him their story.

'We are waiting for the dragon to come up and devour her', they wailed. 'If anybody can save our daughter they will earn our gratitude, the hand of Andromeda and the throne of Ethiopia.'

Perseus found their offer most tempting, as the beauty of the maiden chained to the rock was evident, and the King was rich and prosperous.

He donned the magic helmet of invisibility, which had been given to him by Pluto, the King of the underworld, slipped his arm into the shining shield which had been a present from the goddess Athena (he was related to both these divinities) and, brandishing the diamond sword given to him by the god Mercury, he rushed at the dragon. Since the helmet made Perseus invisible, the monster was unable to defend himself, and Andromeda had no idea who was coming to her rescue. The demigod sliced through the dragon's flesh until he reached the heart and plucked it out. Then he removed his helmet and showed himself to the beautiful princess. With one stroke he cut through the chains that bound her to the rock, and then hoisted the maiden up on to his winged steed and headed for the palace.

On reaching the royal palace, however, an unpleasant surprise was in store for him. Standing at the head of his army was Phineus, Andromeda's former suitor, claiming her as his wife. Perseus, reluctant to give up his well-deserved reward, took out the Medusa's head from a bag, showed it to his enemies and thus turned them to stone. And so he was able to marry the beautiful Andromeda unopposed, and they had many children, one of whom was Alcmena, the mother of the powerful Heracles.

Jason, Medea and the Dragon

J ason was the son and legitimate heir of Aeson, the king of Iolcos, but when he died, the throne was usurped by Aeson's stepbrother Pelias.

Pelias feared that Jason would try to seize the power that was rightfully his and decided to rid himself of the young man, but in such a way that nobody would suspect him. He asked his nephew to bring him the famous golden fleece, which was guarded by a terrible dragon. This golden fleece was the skin of the magic winged ram, sent by the god Hermes to rescue the brother and sister Phrixus and Helle from death. The ram carried them over the sea but Helle fell into the water below, thereafter known as the Hellespont. Phrixus reached Colchis, in Asia Minor. There he sacrificed the animal and gave it to Aeëtes, the King of that land, to thank him for his hospitality. The King of Colchis dedicated the fleece to the god Ares and hung it from a holm-oak, guarded by a dragon.

Obeying his step-uncle's orders, Jason gathered together a group of brave men, and set sail with them aboard a ship called the Argos. The men who took part in the expedition were called the Argonauts, after the ship. When Jason and the heroes of the Argos arrived at Colchis, they told the king that they had come to remove the golden fleece.

Afraid of losing the precious treasure, King Aeëtes did not refuse to hand it over, but he made it a condition that Jason, unaided, must yoke some of the wild bulls of Hephaestus, which breathed fire from their nostrils and had bronze hooves. The hero, dispirited, did not think he could accomplish the task, but the King's daughter Medea was prepared to help him. The princess, who was a skilful sorceress, had fallen in love with the hero and made him promise that if he succeeded in his task thanks to her help, he would marry her and take her back to Greece with him. Jason found the young woman very beautiful and appealing and agreed with alacrity.

Assisted by the clever princess, Jason yoked the bulls of Hephaestus, and, in a second test, defeated some giant warriors. The triumphant hero went to king Aeëtes to demand the golden fleece.

'You've done well,' said the King, 'you have successfully carried out the difficult task I set you. I suspect that you did not do this alone, but you are entitled to try to gain possession of the thing you have come to seek. So go and take the golden fleece, which is hanging from a

tree guarded by a dragon who will not allow anybody to approach. Do not wound him or hurt him in the slightest, for he is a dragon dedicated to the god Ares. You must steal the fleece while he is asleep. That is my last condition.'

The King knew that the clever dragon slept with his eyes open and closed them when he was awake, to deceive the unwary, and he thought that Jason would fall into the trap. However, Medea overheard her father talking about the trick, and gave away the secret to her beloved hero. And so, Jason and the Argonauts waited until night when the monster would open his eyes and sleep. Stealthily they stole the golden fleece and fled to Iolcos aboard the Argos. With them fled Princess Medea, and together they went on to face new dangers.

Cadmus and the Dragon of Ares

Agenor, the king of Tyre and Sidon, had three sons and one very beautiful daughter called Europa. When Zeus, in the form of a bull, carried off Europa, the Syrian king ordered his three sons to set off in search of her and not to return until they had found her.

The three young men set out, but they soon realized the futility of their search. One of the brothers, Cadmus, consulted the oracle at Delphi and the oracle told him to abandon the search for Europa and to found a city. To find the right place, he was to follow a cow until the animal sank down from weariness.

Cadmus travelled on until he reached a lush, fertile valley. It was remote and unpopulated. There, a cow without a yoke was grazing, and Cadmus followed her. The cow lay down to chew the cud near a river, in a beautiful spot, and the young man decided that he would found his city in that very place. Seeing that the prophecy had been fulfilled, he sacrificed the animal to the goddess Athena and then, overcome with exhaustion, he fell asleep.

A beautiful woman dressed in a white tunic appeared to him in his dreams. She was wearing a helmet and a gleaming breastplate. In her hands she held a silver lance and shield, and on her shoulder was perched an owl. Cadmus recognized the goddess Athena.

The apparition spoke softly to him:

'Cadmus, brave warrior, you must indeed found your city here. To do so you must kill an enormous dragon who guards the Spring of Ares. Once you have vanquished him, pull out his teeth and plough a field to sow them.'

The boy prepared to fight the dragon who guarded the Spring of Ares, the god of war. The brave warrior fought a terrible battle against the beast. The powerful dragon used every possible trick, and Cadmus fought valiantly. The ground was soaked with blood, and rocks went flying as though they were pebbles. The yells of the hero and the roaring of the beast could be heard as far away as Mount Olympus, where the din of the contest disturbed the father of the gods who was resting.

Annoyed, Zeus sent his daughter Athena to help Cadmus, and put an end to this racket once and for all.

The goddess of war obediently appeared on the battlefield, but even with her help, it took Cadmus another day to defeat the powerful dragon. After killing the beast, the hero pulled out his teeth. He ploughed a field with great effort, sowed the teeth in the blood-stained and sweat-soaked soil, and waited.

Soon, from the dragon's teeth sprang many fierce warriors, who began to fight among themselves with uncommon determination until there were only five left. The hero then attacked them and disarmed them. The warriors who were called Sparti, 'sown men', then acclaimed Cadmus as their king and lord, and helped him build the walls of the city of Thebes. Thanks to Athena's protection, the heroic Cadmus ruled from then on in that city, which was famous for the valour of her men, for they were born of a dragon's teeth.

Sybaris of Cirfis

Legend has it that on the slopes of Mount Cirfis, close to the city of Delphi, an enormous water dragon called Sybaris came to live. This monster terrorized the local population, for every month she demanded a young, beautiful and innocent adolescent boy, who had not yet tasted the sweetness of love, and devoured him.

Apollo's priests selected the young men to be offered to the dragon, and every month they drew lots to see whose turn it was to be sacrificed.

It so happened that one day fate chose the most beautiful young man of that place, the young Alcyoneus, as Sybaris's victim. In addition to his valour and intelligence, Alcyoneus possessed a beauty which, like Ganymede's, entitled him to serve as cup-bearer to the gods. When the beautiful young man, crowned with roses and looking like a young Apollo, was led amid wailing and chanting to the place of sacrifice, the procession encountered Eurybatus, a brave young warrior. On seeing the beautiful Alcyoneus dressed in a white tunic, the soldier fell madly in love with the young man. He immediately detained the procession and asked:

'Where did you find this boy and where are you taking him?'

'Brave warrior, his destiny is tragic and his future is death,' they replied, 'for he is the victim chosen by Fate to be sacrificed to Sybaris.' Eurybatus turned pale with horror on discovering the boy's destiny and, following the impulse of his heart, asked them to free Alcyoneus and sacrifice him in his place, for his existence would be meaningless if the young man were to die.

'Sacrifice me, for I have lived many years. This young boy has never tasted

86

Fibaris
de
Cirfis

life. Let him enjoy the sun and the love which he deserves, for such a beautiful creature should be a favourite of Eros and Aphrodite, and not of dark Hades.'

The priests did not grant his petition, for they feared that the warrior, who was not as young as the handsome youth, would incur the dragon's wrath against them. But they did allow him to join the procession.

On reaching the place designated by Sybaris for the sacrifice, they all withdrew. Alcyoneus already felt in his heart a profound love for the brave warrior and asked him to take shelter with the others, but the warrior was not prepared to abandon the person who had already become his reason for living. The terrible female dragon came out of the cave thinking she would find a

frightened and defenceless youth, but she met Eurybatus, who, inspired by the love he saw reflected in the eyes of his young companion, launched a surprise attack on the beast and killed her. The dragon was never heard of again and a spring appeared on that spot. Many years later, Eurybatus founded a city in Italy, which he called Sybaris in memory of this feat.

Tannin and the Prophet Daniel

Many, many years ago, several centuries before the birth of Christ, in the sumptuous and pagan Babylon, there lived a young exile from Jerusalem named Daniel. The King of the Babylonians, Nebuchadnezzar, held the young man in high esteem because of his wisdom and he often invited him to his table. Daniel knew how to interpret dreams and his prophecies were always fulfilled, which is why Nebuchadnezzar felt obliged to ask his advice. However, the prophet, who came from the tribe of Judah, was not able to convince the powerful monarch that the stone and metal idols which the Babylonians worshipped were false.

At that time, in the city of Babylon, there lived a dragon called Tannin who was worshipped as a god.

Tannin, who had made a pact of friendship and goodwill with the Babylonians, lived in the temple of Bel, where there were priests and servants to take care of his needs and where the same Nebuchadnezzar often visited him, for he was an ancient and wise dragon.

One day, when Daniel had demonstrated to the Babylonian monarch the falsity of the god Bel, Nebuchadnezzar asked him angrily:

'And why don't you worship the dragon god? You cannot deny that the dragon is alive. He is not made of stone or metal like the other gods in this land.'

'He is alive but he is not a god, for he can die and gods do not die', replied the prophet.

'He has been alive since the time when my father and his father were young, and even long before. He has lived in the

temple for countless generations of men, and there is nobody who remembers when he was born. He eats and drinks and speaks with wisdom, and he is very knowledgeable. I do not imagine or believe that he will ever die. He is without a doubt a god', retorted Nebuchadnezzar.

Daniel then wanted to demonstrate to the King that the dragon could die and was therefore no different from other creatures. He made cakes of pitch and sheep's fat and wool, and gave them to the poor, trusting Tannin, who, accustomed to being given food by men, did not suspect anything and ate them.

The poisoned cakes soon began to work and the dragon died in two days. Thus the king of the Babylonians was convinced that Tannin was mortal, and he lost his wise dragon god forever.

The Dragon Prince

In the high Middle Ages, the most renowned tournaments of poetry in all of France were held at the court of Eleanor of Aquitaine. Celebrated troubadours gathered there to demonstrate their art, and once a year the winner of this poetic joust was announced.

On one occasion, the winner was an unknown and very handsome young man, who refused to give his name or say where he came from, despite the entreaties of Eleanor herself. The aura of mystery surrounding the anonymous troubadour, together with his kindness and beauty, soon made him one of the favourites among the ladies of the court. Griselda, a young and wistful maiden, the youngest daughter of the lord of Foix, fell passionately in love with the knight and declared her love for him. Moved by the maiden's entreaties, the troubadour agreed to marry her in secret and take her to his home, but on condition that Griselda should never try to see him other than when he chose, and that she should never try to discover his secret.

The lovesick lady promised to comply with this strange condition. It seemed little to ask in exchange for being able to remain with her loved one.

One night, the young Griselda had fallen asleep in the arms of her lover in the castle of Eleanor of Aquitaine where she lived, and on opening her eyes she found herself in an unfamiliar room. It was a luxurious place, adorned with silk and precious stones, and beside her lay her husband smiling benignly at her.

'You are in my house, which belongs to you', said the troubadour. 'You may give orders to my servants and do whatever you please. There are stables with horses at your disposal, huntsmen and hawks for hunting, and you may come and go as you wish. You are my lady, and all that is mine is yours. There are maidens ready to serve you and to carry out your every whim, dancers and musicians to entertain you, jewels and silks to adorn you. If you need anything, tell me and I will give it to you.'

'I wish only for the love of my lord', replied the young woman, bewildered.

'That is good, my love, but do not forget your promise.'

Griselda, full of happiness, demonstrated her compliance by flinging herself into the arms of her beloved husband.

For a while the lady kept her promise and believed she was in paradise. The troubadour knight, who was kind and passionate, spent most of his time with his wife. Occasionally he would disappear into a locked room, and she, faithful to her promise, did not ask him any questions. However, curiosity gradually got the better of her. One day she decided to find out the secret of her knight. She crept up to the door of the forbidden room, which he had left ajar, and spied through the chink. Horrified, she watched as the troubadour turned into a huge dragon with green scales and powerful wings. She could not prevent a cry of horror escaping her lips. The dragon prince wheeled round, and saw his terrified wife in the doorway. Deeply hurt by this betrayal, the knight bade his servants remove Griselda immediately to the court of Aquitaine, and never again did he return to see her.

The lady could not forget her beloved, and not a day went by without her recalling the months of happiness beside the gentle dragon. Full of repentance and sadness, she wrote down her adventure; that is how the famous story of the dragon prince has found its way to us.

Jilocasin

During the reign of Charlemagne, there lived in the region of Gascony a very old and wise dragon called Jilocasin, who was a poet. Every so often, Jilocasin would abandon his comfortable and spacious dwelling and take on a human form to visit the King's court. There he was a well-known and respected troubadour, and he made the most of these brief sojourns to sing his verses and listen to the creations of other poets. Then he would return to his home in Gascony, where he could compose in peace and lead a peaceful life far from the world.

One day, he was travelling through the forests of Gascony disguised as a troubadour, when he heard a desperate cry for help. Without losing a moment he ran in the direction of the screams and came across a poor woman who was trying to defend herself against some bandits. Jilocasin changed back into a dragon and with two blows he finished off the ruffians. The woman had fainted from her injuries, and the dragon lifted her onto his back and flew speedily back to his dwelling.

Jilocasin's servants took care of the lady, whose clothes, although they were torn and dirty, were those of a lady of high rank.

On undoing the bundle which the woman clasped to her breast, they found a baby only a few weeks old slumbering peacefully, oblivious to everything.

Thanks to the care and solicitude of the servants, the woman soon came to, and Jilocasin took on his human shape to visit his protegée. The lady expressed her gratitude and told him her story. She had been widowed within two years of marriage, and her family had forced her to marry her cousin, an unscrupulous man who was interested only in inheriting the title and wealth of her deceased husband.

The wedding was celebrated in haste, before the mourning period prescribed by law had been observed.

'But I was pregnant by my first husband, something which my cousin did not know', explained the woman, weeping. 'When the baby was born, six months after the forced wedding, my husband tried to seize the baby to prevent him threatening his inheritance. Fearing for the life of my son, I ran away, but the villain pursued me with his henchmen, and he almost succeeded in killing the child.

Fortunately, you saved us, and now my life belongs to you.'

Touched by the grief and beauty of the woman, Jilocasin offered her support and shelter in his house.

Time passed, and the dragon-troubadour and the lady became inseparable. The beautiful fugitive was aware of Jilocasin's true identity, but she was so taken by his kindness and amiability that it did not affect her love for him. Meanwhile, the dragon found in her the understanding and friendship he had always sought. Jilocasin and the lady would go for long walks together, and sometimes the dragon would carry her on his back and they would visit far-off lands. Together they rode, loved, and sang the verses which the dragon-poet

composed. They spent three happy years in this way. To complete her happiness, the woman became pregnant. They were both looking forward to the birth of their son, but the lady died in childbirth. Jilocasin was inconsolable. He had lost an irreplaceable companion, the only woman who loved him as he was.

Faithful to her memory, the dragon cared for the two boys without making any distinction between his adoptive son and his own son. He taught them the highest principles and, after a while, presented them at court to be armed knights.

The two brothers, who chose to be called the Knights of the Dragon, were famous for their nobility and honour, and they finally avenged their mother's memory by capturing the castle which their villainous uncle had stolen from them.

Tristan and the Fire Dragon

A long time ago, in the dark and heroic years of the Middle Ages, a terrible Fire Dragon settled in Ireland, terrorizing the population on his nocturnal forays during which he burned everything he came across.

In desperation, the King of Ireland publicly declared that he would give the hand of his daughter, the fair Iseult, to the knight who could deliver his country from the beast.

At that time, there was a young knight at the Irish court called Tristan, who was

there as a messenger from his uncle, King Mark of Cornwall, to ask for the hand of the beautiful Iseult for his King. The young man did not hold out much hope of accomplishing his mission, for the King of Cornwall was advanced in years, and he doubted that the beautiful princess would consider him a good match. On hearing the royal declaration, Tristan thought that if he could kill the dragon the maiden would be his and he could take her to King Mark.

Knowing that water was fatal for fire dragons, Tristan took a wine skin full of water and hung it over the door to the monster's lair. Then he lay in wait for the dragon to come out.

So fierce was the dragon and so many deaths had he caused that not even the most valiant knight in the kingdom dared challenge him. However, the major-domo of the royal household, who nursed a secret passion for the princess Iseult, was hiding near the cave, watching to see what would happen. The crafty steward had no intention of killing the beast, he was much too afraid, but he was certain that by using his wits, he would be able to take advantage of the exploits of some brave knight and receive the credit for killing the dragon himself.

From his hiding place, the astonished major-domo saw an unknown youth present himself before the monster's cave and call him in a loud voice.

When the dragon appeared, the wine skin full of water fell on him and quenched his fire. Then, a fierce struggle began between the knight and the dragon.

At last, after long hours of gruelling combat, Tristan managed to kill the monster, but was so exhausted that he only had the strength to cut out and keep the dragon's tongue before losing consciousness.

At the sight of the slain dragon and the senseless knight lying on the ground, the treacherous steward decided to turn the situation to his advantage. With one stroke he cut off the monster's head and presented himself to the king as the author of the deed, claiming the promised reward. Iseult was in great despair, for she did not desire the old major-domo for a husband. She could not believe that the steward had succeeded in such a difficult task, and the princess paid a secret visit to the dragon's cave.

When she reached it and saw the unconscious young man, Iseult understood that they had been tricked. She liked the knight's handsome features and, as she did not know of Tristan's plans, she sent her servants to bring back the wounded man in secret to the palace, where she tenderly cared for him.

Two days later, the court gathered to announce officially that the dragon had been slain and to give the triumphant major-domo the princess's hand. Proud as a peacock the steward of the royal household stood at the foot of the throne

waiting for his reward. Iseult, dressed in gold and silver sat next to the King, and the room was thronged with countless courtiers decked out in their finery. The King had not yet spoken when Tristan burst into the room and asked for the hand of the princess.

'By what right do you ask for her hand?' asked the King, furiously.

'By the right of my sword and as the slayer of the dragon, Your Majesty', replied the young man. The court burst out laughing, but the fury of the Irish lord was evident.

'You presumptuous young man, perhaps you are unaware that the major-domo has killed the monster?' Then the beautiful princess broke in, for she could not help thinking that the unknown knight was much handsomer and that his kisses would be much sweeter than those of the steward.

'Let him explain, father, I implore you.'

'Very well,' agreed the King, 'let the stranger speak.'

'Let the dragon's tongue speak for me', retorted Tristan.

'The dragon is dead, you impudent young man, how can he speak?'

'Look in his mouth, your majesty', replied the hero.

The steward was thrown into confusion when they opened the monster's mouth and saw that his tongue was missing.

'Here is the missing tongue', and Tristan showed the astonished courtiers and the smiling Iseult the tongue of the animal which he had kept.

And so the major-domo's trick was discovered, and he was severely punished for his treason. The King declared Tristan the winner and then Tristan announced that he did not claim the princess's hand for himself, but for his uncle, Mark of Cornwall. The monarch was delighted at the news, for the King of Cornwall was rich and much appreciated by the Irish court. As for Iseult, she did not allow herself to be too disappointed by this announcement, for she had decided to win the heart of the valiant knight. The legend tells how Tristan also fell in love with the beautiful princess, and this love led to a sad tale in which the two lovers ended up dying, unable to part.

The Peasant and the Dragon

One day, a dragon who was flying back home was caught in a violent storm. The wind howled and the rain came down with such force that even the sturdiest oak trees were uprooted and blown down like straw. Despite his great size, the dragon was buffeted in all directions and in the end he lost his way in the dark. In vain he tried and tried again to rise above the storm, battling with all his strength against the elements, but at last, overcome with weariness, he fell exhausted to the ground.

While he lay unconscious in the mud, a peasant who lived in a humble shack nearby walked past.

On catching sight of the monster, who lay so still that he looked dead, the man, whose name was Lucas, felt sorry for him. He approached the inert body and saw that the dragon was still alive. With the help of his horse he moved the dragon to an outhouse which served as a barn. Then he made the dragon comfortable and covered him with a patched blanket, and ran into the house to ask his wife to prepare some hot food. She was apprehensive.

'You are mad if you want to give food and shelter to such a beast. You would do better to kill him and then the king will give us a reward for his skin.'

'Quiet woman,' retorted Lucas. 'The dragon is weak and ill, and it is not Christian to deny help to the ailing, of

102

whatever race they belong to.'

'Don't be stupid husband!' exclaimed his wife. 'This creature is not a Christian, nor is he a man. He will eat you the minute he is better.'

Taking no notice of his wife's warning, the peasant devoted himself to feeding and caring for the animal. As a result of his efforts, the dragon soon recovered and thanked the peasant for saving him.

'There is nothing to thank me for', replied the good man. 'We are all God's creatures.'

'Even so, many men in your position would have killed me and sold my skin, which is very valuable.'

'Any man who takes advantage of the fallen must be very evil. Such behaviour does not befit a knight', replied the peasant.

On hearing her husband's words, the wife, who was listening at the door, began to laugh.

'Look at this fool, giving himself the airs of a knight when he is a pauper!' she exclaimed from her hiding place. 'You won't speak like that when the tax collectors come and take away our horse because we haven't paid our taxes.'

'It is honour not wealth that makes a man a knight', replied the worthy Lucas in a low voice.

However, the dragon heard the conversation, and, noting the peasant's poverty, offered him a reward for his trouble.

'I could not refuse anything in gold, because the tax collector is coming soon and I have nothing to pay him with. But that is not why I helped you, friend', said the man.

'I know, but now that I am strong

enough to fly home, come to my cave and choose anything you wish. Lucas climbed fearlessly onto the dragon's back, but his wife begged him not to trust the dragon.

'When you are in the middle of the forest, he will eat you,' she groaned', and I will be left alone.'

The dragon bore the peasant to his cave and there he entertained him for three days. When the time came for him to return home, the animal loaded a huge sack of gold and precious stones on to his back as a gift, and carried Lucas back to his shack.

'Come and see me whenever you are hard up', he said on parting.

Lucas found his wife sad and dressed in mourning, for she believed he was dead. With the dragon's gifts the couple were able to buy a beautiful farm with many animals, but the wife started becoming extravagant, and one day she said to her husband:

'If we had a little more money, we would be able to buy good land and employ others to work on it, and then when we have a son he will be able to be a knight. Why don't you ask the dragon for a little more gold?' Lucas refused, but in the end he gave in and went to see the dragon. The creature thought it was a sound idea, and was delighted to be able to help his friend once more. But then hardly a year went by and the wife insisted:

'If we could buy a castle and some villages, we would become counts.' Lucas, tired of his wife's nagging, went once more to see the dragon in his cave, and the latter granted his request. The couple received a dukedom. Not long

afterwards, the wife wanted to go and live at court.

One day, the new duchess saw the queen arriving in her golden carriage, dressed in silks, with silver farthingales, and wearing fabulous jewels.

Her eyes glinting with ambition, she said:

'My good Lucas, it has occurred to me that when we have a son, if there is a war he will have to go to the front as an officer, and he might die in combat. It would be much better if we became monarchs so that our son would be in less danger. Your friend the dragon will grant us this wish.'

'But wife don't talk nonsense.' His wife cried and entreated him until finally Lucas decided to visit the dragon who greeted him warmly.

'Friend,' said the dragon after listening to his story, 'your wife is too ambitious. She will never leave you in peace. She will never have enough and she will always want more, but I have the answer. Come into the cave.'

And the dragon showed his guest into a cosy room where beautiful young women were singing and dancing.

'Now you are my prisoner. These girls will keep you company and will see that your every wish is carried out, for they are my slaves, but you will not be able to leave the cave other than in my company and you will not return to see your wife.'

From then on the good man lived happily with the dragon and the maidens. As for Lucas's wife, she had to dress in mourning, convinced that her husband had finally been devoured by the monster, just as she had predicted from the beginning.

The Cuelebre

In a hut in an Asturian village lived a very beautiful maiden, who was vain and forever daydreaming. She spent hours and hours combing her long flowing hair by a spring, and there was nothing she loved more than to admire her beautiful reflection in the limpid water of the pool. In vain her mother and grandmother warned her:

'It is dangerous to comb your hair by the spring. Be careful, because if a hair falls and ruffles the surface of the water, the spirit of the spring will bewitch you.'

'Old wives tales,' cried the girl, 'there is no spirit in the fountain.' But the girl was very wrong. In this pool lived a very powerful spirit, one of those nymphs of the streams and mountains which abound in Asturian mythology. The spirit watched angrily as the girl spent the whole day combing her hair, never helping to spin the wool or knead the dough. She had not been able to do a thing about it, as the girl did not ruffle the water of the pool, but patiently the nymph waited for her chance.

Then, one day, one of the girl's golden hairs fell into the water and the nymph, dressed in a cloak of green water, rose angrily out of the pool.

'Didn't your mother warn you not to ruffle the water?' she asked, in a very quiet voice.

'A hair as beautiful as this does not ruffle the water', replied the proud maiden.

'I am going to bewitch you to punish you for your pride', the spirit said icily. Barefoot, her long golden hair adorned with pearls and a crown made from the reflection of the moon, she alighted on the grass next to the pool. Frowning, she declared: 'I am turning you into a cuelebre. You will only turn back into a maiden if you meet a knight who is so brave that he is not afraid of you and has a heart so pure that he finds you beautiful.

At once the girl's body grew to an enormous size and became covered with coloured scales. Her golden hair turned into crests and two wings sprouted from her shoulders. With a howl of despair, the cuelebre slunk off weeping, and hid in a cave by the sea.

As all the youths who set eyes on the cuelebre are afraid, the proud girl who was bewitched by the spirit of the spring still lives in her little cave on the sea shore, waiting for the knight who will find her beautiful, so that she can become a maiden once more.

The Tarasque

There is an ancient legend that tells how, in the high Middle Ages, there lived in a lake in the south of France a huge blue water dragon covered in steely scales, known as the Tarasque. The local population was terrorized by the presence of the monster, who would emerge from the lake from time to time to devour a virgin, as is customary among water dragons.

The villagers did not know what to do to free themselves of the Tarasque. Nobody was brave enough to fight against the beast, nor was there anyone who would dare even speak with him to negotiate a truce. In the end, the people decided to send emissaries to the court of the King of France, but the King had other more serious problems to deal with and was not interested in the troubles of a village so far from the capital. Nor were the knights of the court interested in the problem. The dragon did not guard any treasure that would make the challenge worth their while, nor was he holding a princess prisoner whom they could free to gain honour and glory. 'The dragon only devours humble ignorant and filthy peasants. The tournaments and jousts are much more profitable', thought the 'valiant' knights.

In desperation, the local people gathered to discuss the possibility of abandoning the village, given that they were unable to rid themselves of the monster. The discussions were becoming heated when St Martha, a beautiful young woman who was known and worshipped in the region for her goodness and bounty, happened to be passing that way.

The village elders interpreted her appearance as a sign from the heavens and went to meet her to ask for her help, desperately beseeching her. In response

to the villagers' urgent entreaties, the young woman offered to capture the Tarasque, but on one condition.

'Tell us what you require, good Saint', agreed the local people.

'I just want you to pray to God for three days, asking Him to help me overcome the Tarasque', replied Martha.

The elders accepted her condition, and waited full of faith that a miracle would happen which would save them forever from the curse.

So, one morning, the Saint made her way to the lake where the Tarasque lived. The dragon was a great music lover despite his ferocity.

The beautiful young woman stood on the shore and began singing praises to God and to the Virgin Mary in a beautiful passionate voice. Enchanted by the sweetness of the song, the Tarasque came out of the water and lay down at Martha's feet. The Saint quickly tied a belt around his neck without the monster offering the slightest resistance. The dragon was completely subdued, and Martha was able to lead him easily to the village, where he was killed by the peasants. In memory of this feat, the region where the Tarasque lived was known after that as Tarascon.

La Vibria

The history books tell us that when Count Jofre el Pilós governed most of the Catalonian territories, there lived in a cave in the Massif of Sant Llorenç, near the town of Terrassa, a monstrous dragon known as La Vibria.

When he was still young, the dragon was put in the cave by the Moors, who wanted to avenge themselves on the Christians for expelling them from the region. The animal grew until he became a powerful beast, who, on his nocturnal forays into the surrounding countryside, devoured flocks and shepherds, devastated the farms and terrorized the local people. The town of Terrassa offered a substantial reward to whoever could free them from this terrible menace. Many knights, monks and soldiers tried to kill the Vibria, but as he was a cunning dragon who was very well versed in magic, nobody succeeded in subduing him.

Finally, Count Jofre, tired of the monster's excesses and of his subjects' complaints, decided to confront him. Fully armed, and riding his powerful black steed, the Count set out for the dragon's cave. The place was deserted, and only a black rook was perched on a branch. But the brave Jofre was not taken in by the Vibria's tricks and he called him by his name:

'Vibria!'

The dragon immediately abandoned his bird disguise and turned into a horrendous winged beast who seized the Count with his sharp talons and tried to lift him off the ground and dash him against the rocks. Without flinching, Jofre lashed out bravely against the dragon's scaly neck, and, when the beast opened his enormous jaws, he plunged his sword down his gullet, wounding him fatally. However, the dragon still managed to fly off, but he fell headlong on to the mountain side, which has been known ever since by the name of Puig de la Creu (the Peak of the Cross).

The Count founded a convent of monks near the cave, and on the summit of the moutain he had a monastery built, so that never again would a dragon make his home among the rocks where the Vibria had lived.

Count Jofre's battle against the Vibria is recorded for posterity on the sculpted door of Sant Iu, in Barcelona Cathedral, where it can still be seen today.

The Dragon of Mont Blanc

The peaceful little town of Mont Blanc was a contented place. It was governed by a good wise king and had a healthy economy. The King had a very beautiful daughter who was loved and respected by all. The only cloud on the horizon was that the inhabitants of the town were not sufficiently pious and they often forgot to offer up gifts to the gods, which considerably angered the pagan priests.

Legend has it that one midsummer's day an enormous dragon with brilliant greeny-blue scales rose out of the river. The horrendous beast appeared before the terrorized population and spoke to them thus:

'Every month you must bring me a beautiful young virgin for my food,' he crooned in a sing-song voice, 'otherwise I will destroy your homes and your fields, your crops and all your livestock. If you obey me, I promise I will not attack anybody and I will allow you to live in peace.'

The terrified townsfolk ran to the palace to tell the King of their misfortune. Much to his sorrow, he had to accept the dragon's conditions. In vain the population entreated the gods to liberate them from the terrible monster, and in vain the priests of the pagan cults offered up sacrifices and gifts to the gods begging them to rid the town of the menace. Months went by, and every new moon a young virgin was handed over to the starving dragon.

The situation became unbearable. In the homes where they were not weeping over a dead daughter, they feared for the fate of their children, and girls were flinging themselves into the arms of the first man they met so they would no longer be virgins. Girls designated as future victims had to be locked up and heavily guarded to prevent them from killing themselves to avoid their terrible fate.

After a while, there were no virgins left, and the only people who were pleased were the pagan priests, because the people were returning to religion and making offerings to the gods.

The month of April came, almost a year since the arrival of the monster. Fate's next victim was the King's daughter, who had insisted on taking part in the lottery of young girls destined to be sacrificed.

Resigned to her misfortune, the girl, who not long before had converted to Christianity, spent the night in prayer, and in the morning, attired in a white tunic and crowned with flowers, she bade farewell to her grief-stricken parents and the weeping villagers. With a strength of mind inspired by her faith, and trusting completely in the Virgin Mary, the girl made her way alone to the dragon's cave and calmly awaited her end, praying all the while.

The legend describes how the townsfolk gathered along the city walls to wait for the monster to come out of his cave, and to witness the imminent tragedy. Suddenly an unknown knight arrived, galloping furiously on a white charger with a silver mane. It is said that his weapons shone like silver and his cloak was as red as glowing embers. His shield was emblazoned with a red cross on a gold background.

Without dismounting or reining-in his horse, the stranger charged at the beast. Overwhelmed by the power of the magnificent horseman, the dragon retreated and tamely lay down.

'My lady,' said the stranger, 'tie the belt from your tunic around the dragon's neck and he will follow us meekly.'

The girl fearlessly carried out his instructions, and the animal allowed himself to be led away without offering any resistance.

The strange procession made its way to the gates of the town, where the inhabitants were waiting in astonishment.

The girl ran to embrace her parents, while the pagan priests boasted that they had defeated the monster with their

offerings and rituals.

The knight asked for silence and the whole town listened to the words of the mysterious and valiant saviour.

'I am George, the soldier of Christ,' he said, 'and I am devoted to Him. This young Christian girl prayed for help from Mary and her son, the Redeemer, and that is why I was given the mission of saving her from death. May the cross which saved you crown this town forever. Abandon your false idols and you need never fear the dragon again.'

And to confirm his words, the young knight traced the sign of the cross above the docile monster. Immediately, the animal was transformed into a rosebush with roses as red as blood.

Still today, in Catalonia, the name of Saint George is associated with red roses, as a reminder of the knight who rid them of the terrible dragon forever.

Siegfried and Fafnir

Odin, the father of the gods, told the giants to build a beautiful bridge to unite Valhalla, the celestial paradise, with the Earth. The builders demanded in return Freyja, the goddess of beauty.

When the bridge was finished, the gods wanted to rescue Freyja from the giants, but the giants demanded a suitable ransom: the treasure which the Nibelung dwarves hoarded with the Rhine gold. And so the gods were forced to steal the dwarves' treasure and hand it over to the giants, who hoarded it in a cave guarded by the dragon Fafnir.

Mimi, one of the dwarves, was desperate, for the dwarves could do nothing against the dragon. When he learned that Sigmund, King and hero of the Volsung, had died in battle, he decided to take charge of the now fatherless little Prince Siegfried and turn him into a warrior as brave and strong as the deceased king. The dwarf became the prince's tutor, with the intention of getting him to steal the treasure guarded by the dragon.

When Siegfried reached the age of eighteen, Mimi gave him the broken fragments of his father's sword, the magic Gram, and taught him how to forge the sword anew. When the sword was whole again, the dwarf told Siegfried about the dragon Fafnir, but not about the treasure.

'It would be a great exploit, young Siegfried, if a prince as strong and brave as you succeeded in killing the dragon', said Mimi, to entice him. The bold Siegfried agreed to undertake this task and lost no time in making his way to the dragon's cave. On arriving at the monster's lair, he called him loudly.

Fafnir awoke and came out, intending to devour the thoughtless intruder. Fearlessly, the hero brandished the magic Gram and withstood the attack, and when the dragon reared his enormous head, he plunged the sword into the beast's neck.

Mortally wounded in the jugular, the beast collapsed in a pool of blood, and a few drops splashed Siegfried's lips, giving him the wonderful faculty of understanding the language of the birds:

'Here's young Siegfried who has just killed the dragon. If he were to bathe in the monster's blood, he would become invulnerable', sang some birds.

'He is not as clever as he seems if he doesn't realize that Mimi will betray him. The dwarf only wanted the treasure that Fafnir was guarding and now that the dragon is dead, he will kill Siegfried', cheeped others. The young man followed the birds' advice and bathed in the dragon's blood. From then on he was invulnerable. However, a lime leaf fell on his shoulder while he was bathing, and this tiny little patch of his body was not protected by the magic blood.

Then, Siegfried killed the artful Mimi, who only wanted the treasure, and went into the dragon's cave. The hero, whom the birds continued to advise, kept the magic helmet of invisibility and the dwarf's ring, which he found among the precious objects in the cave. After this exploit, he sheathed the powerful Gram and set off in search of new adventures.

118

The Gypsy and the Dragon

In the vast steppes of Russia there lived a tribe of gypsies, who travelled up and down the country selling remedies and beads, never staying for long in the same place. The leader was an astute and sharp-witted man whose name was Yuri, and he had six clever sons. One day, when the tribe was camped next to a town celebrating the holiday of Saint Basil, Yuri was told that a few versts from there lived a moujik who was selling colts at a very good price. The astute gypsy thought that he would be able to do a good deal if he bought the animals and then sold them again, and he set out cheerfully. He put a piece of fresh cheese and slice of rye bread in a pouch and made his way to the moujik's village, leaving his people to sell their wares at the fair.

On arriving in the neighbouring village, he was surprised to find the place silent and deserted. He walked through the narrow streets in astonishment, looking for clues as to what had happened. Suddenly, he heard a terrified voice warning him:

'Flee from here wretch, if you don't want the dragon to devour you.'

'Who is speaking?' asked Yuri.

'It is I, old Vestia.' And from behind some filthy willow baskets emerged an old man with a long beard. He was stooped and trembling, and so thin that he was nothing more than skin and bone.

'Hello, granddad,' said Yuri amiably, 'what is going on here?'

'Oh, my son!' sighed the old man, 'an evil dragon has devoured all the inhabitants of the town ... people, animals, even the cats! I am the only person left because I am so old that the monster didn't fancy eating skin and bones, but today he will return, and as he will find nothing else to eat, he will eat me too. Go far from here, if you do not want to suffer the same fate.'

'Don't worry granddad,' replied the bold Yuri. 'I am not afraid of the dragon. If you do what I tell you no harm will befall you. Hide among the willow baskets and don't say a word.'

Soon the earth began to shake from the dragon's footsteps. He was enormous and looked very hungry.

Yuri, who knew that dragons are vain and curious by nature, went up to him and greeted him courteously:

'Good day, tsar of the dragons.'

The dragon was very proud to be addressed thus. He thrashed the ground with his tail, spread his wings to display the marvellous jewelled breastplate adorning his chest and bowed his head, saying modestly:

'But that is not so, I am simply a common dragon.'

'You are not common, magnificent lord,' protested Yuri, 'you are the greatest, the most beautiful and the most powerful of all. I am eager to admire your strength.'

'Yes,' admitted the vain animal, coiling and uncoiling his tail, blushing with pleasure, 'it's true I am strong and I am generally thought beautiful. But who are you standing before me so fearlessly?'

'I am the strongest man in the world,' replied Yuri with alacrity.

'You are the strongest? Don't make me laugh!'

'But I am, even though you doubt my words.'

The dragon, who by now was very interested in the gypsy, picked up a stone and crushed it to powder.

'Perhaps you can do the same, if you are the strongest of humans.'

'That wouldn't be difficult,' replied Yuri with aplomb, 'but can you squeeze water out of the stone as I can?' And without letting the dragon see what he picked up from his pouch, he squeezed the fresh cheese until the whey trickled out between his fingers.

'Well,' thought the dragon, 'he really is very strong. It would be better to have him as a friend than an enemy.'

And to win the man's friendship he suggested:

'Come and eat at my house. You are a very nice human being and I would like us to be friends.'

'Very well dragon, let's go.' The monster took Yuri to the cave where he lived and asked him:

'Would you kindly go to the woods and bring back an oak tree to make a fire.'

Yuri went out determined to prevent the dragon from discovering the trick, but his arms were not strong enough to uproot such enormous trees and bring them back to the cave. Then he had an idea and he tied a group of sturdy oaks together with the rope the dragon had given him.

After a while, and seeing that the gypsy had not returned, the animal made his way to the woods and met Yuri who was very busy tying the trunks carefully together.

'What on earth are you doing?' asked the reptile, astonished.

'Well, I thought that if I bring back all the trees at once we will have wood for several days.'

'Leave it, leave it, we don't want to cut down the whole wood', replied the dragon, more and more convinced of his friend's strength. 'I'll take the trunk back home. Meanwhile, bring me a bullock to cook. Behind the house, in a field, you will find a fine herd of bullocks. Just make sure you choose the plumpest.'

Yuri set off determinedly for the field, and after a while the dragon found him tying the bullocks together.

'What are you doing?'

'Well I thought if I brought all the bullocks back to the cave we could make a big bullock stew.'

'Friend,' said the dragon sighing, 'you have a strange way of doing things. One bullock will be enough. I'll take him back myself.' And somewhat perturbed by his guest's behaviour, the dragon seized the plumpest bullock, killed it, skinned it and started to cook it. The two friends gorged themselves until they were full, and after the sumptuous feast, the dragon, who was in a good mood, offered to accompany the gypsy back to his house.

'Thank you,' replied Yuri, 'but I was thinking of buying some horses.'

'Don't worry about that, I have a beautiful colt, and I can sell it to you for a hundred roubles.'

Yuri agreed to the deal and told the dragon that he would pay him when they reached his house. As it was a long way the dragon decided to adopt a human form. They set out on horses belonging to the dragon and made good progress towards the camp. During the journey, Yuri warned his friend that he had six sons who were strong and had clairvoyant powers. When they reached the outskirts of the camp, Yuri's sons ran to meet him, and on seeing the colt they began to shout.

'You've only brought one!'

'It must be for me', shouted the oldest.

'No, no, I want this one', argued the smallest.

Yuri looked at the dragon and said:

'What rascals! Didn't I tell you that they were clairvoyant? They have recognized you.' The dragon, terrified, thought that the boys wanted to keep him as a plaything, or to devour him, and as they were as strong as their father, there was no possible hope of escape for him. He quickly dismounted from his horse, took on his dragon form and flew off in a panic. Never again did he dare go near the Russian Steppes, where the gypsies are so strong they fight over dragons.

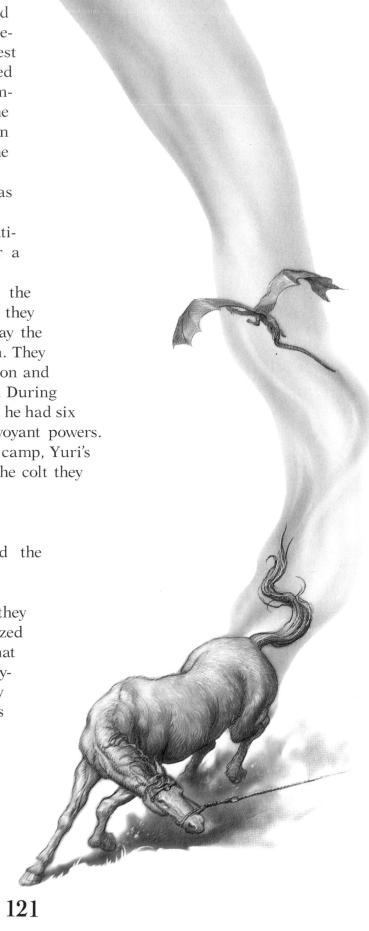

Dragons in Modern Literature

The dragons of the Dragonlance legends are majestic and terrifying creatures, whose principal attraction is perhaps their great age. They are divided between good and evil, without the ambiguity or callousness typical of most of the other characters in this book.

The benign and the perverse dragons are equally beautiful and powerful, the only difference is in their actions.

The good dragons are differentiated externally by their metallic bronze, silver and golden scales. The bronze dragons are bellicose, but also sociable, as demonstrated by Khirsah and Flamestrike. The golden dragons, who are haughty and majestic, are more akin to gods than humans; their main exponent is Pyros, Ansalon is the most ancient and their most assiduous mount is Fizban, the incarnation of the god of Good. However, the silver dragons are those which hold the greatest fascination for the reader.

Let us remember, for example, the silver woman-dragon who accompanies the hero Huma in his odyssey, or Silvara the elfin seductress who had a beautiful but tormented love affair with Prince Gilthanas.

As for the dragons of evil, they all have similar colouring: white, green, blue, red and black scales. Noteworthy among the white dragons is Sleet, the guardian of the Wall of Ice, while prominent among the green dragons is Cyan Bloodbane, who created nightmares in the mind of the elf king Lorac until he went completely mad. The principal black dragon is Onyx, the ferocious guardian of the Disks of Mishakal, in the ruins of Xak Tsaroth. Meanwhile the squadrons of red and blue dragons mostly take part in great battles. Distinguished red dragons include Ember, the mount of the evil Verminaard, and Flamestrike, also known as Matafleur, the 'maternal' female who kills a fellow dragon in the battle of Pax Tharkas herself and dies.

Of the blue dragons, the most memorable is Skie, the loyal companion of Kitiara, the feared and evil dark queen, who was responsible for the death of the brave noble Sturm Brightblade.

The gods of the Dragonlance also sometimes adopted reptilian forms: Paladine, the god of Good, is the great platinum dragon, and Takhisis, the queen of darkness, turns into a five-headed dragon who personifies and perpetuates the infernal pleiad.

Nor should we forget a species peculiar to this saga and directly related to the dragons, the draconians. A perversion of the Sons of Good, these creatures hatched from eggs which the evil reptiles stole from their good brothers. Bewitched at birth by a black witch, the draconians constitute an aberrant sub-species of the most distinguished creatures that populate the world of Krynn.

Dragons in the World of J.R.R. Tolkien

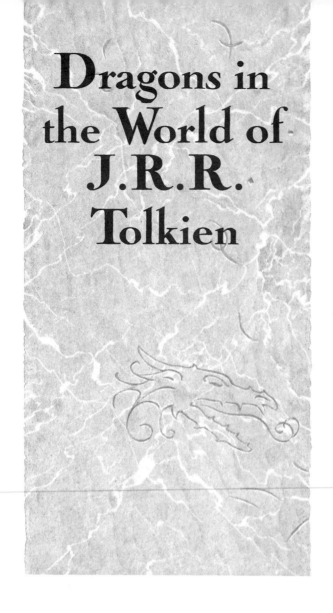

There are no good dragons in Middle Earth. The impressive reptiles in Tolkien's fantasy are perverse and destructive with a number of fundamental characteristics: they possess significant magic powers, they can live for thousands of years and are greedy and arrogant – faults which make them vulnerable. They also have very sharp eyesight and a keen sense of smell, and in general they possess considerable physical abilities.

There are different classes of dragon, but the main distinction resides in whether or not they can fly. Within each of these two species, we encounter fire dragons, capable of projecting enormous flames from their mouths, and dragons of the cold, with icy breath which freezes their victims. The origin of these terrible creatures can be found in the epic *The Silmarillion*, published after the death of Tolkien, which recounts the whole history of his imaginary Middle Earth. In this work we read about beings created in the First Age by Morgoth. The first to appear in the chronicles was Glaurung, a fire dragon who could not

fly. Glaurung took part in the Battle of the Sudden Flame and in the Battle of the Unnumbered Tears and was finally killed by the hero Túrin.

However, the most terrible of these creatures was Ancalagon the Black, an immense winged fire dragon, who died in the War of Wrath, felled by a well-aimed arrow shot from Eärendil, while he was fighting against the great eagles. It is said that when he fell, the impact of his gigantic body against the mountains of Beleriand caused a cataclysm which changed the geography of Middle Earth.

After the War of Wrath, during the second and third Ages, the dragons took refuge in the remote north, in the region known as the Dead Marshes, or in caves in the Misty Mountains. From there, from time to time, they descended south and brought chaos and destruction in their wake.

Of all those who remained in Middle Earth, the greatest and the most famous was Smaug, who was also a winged fire dragon. At the end of the Third Age, he devastated the kingdom of the dwarves in Erebor, the lonely mountain, and

seized the vast treasure. How and why is told in *The Hobbit*, where the dwarf Thorin Oakenshield organizes an expedition to recover the treasure stolen by Smaug and to avenge the destruction the dragon wreaked on the dwarves. He fulfills his aim when the Hobbit, Bilbo Baggins, manages to trick the dragon and helps Bardo, a human hero, to kill him.

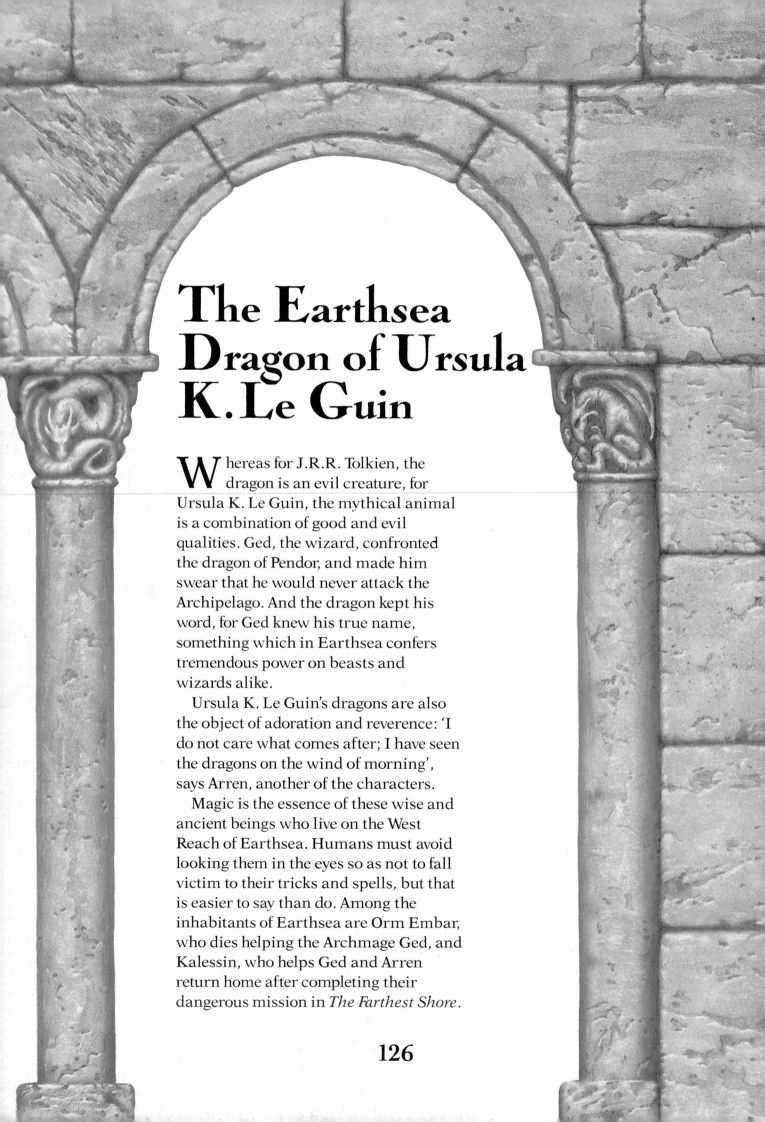

The Earthsea Dragon of Ursula K. Le Guin

Whereas for J.R.R. Tolkien, the dragon is an evil creature, for Ursula K. Le Guin, the mythical animal is a combination of good and evil qualities. Ged, the wizard, confronted the dragon of Pendor, and made him swear that he would never attack the Archipelago. And the dragon kept his word, for Ged knew his true name, something which in Earthsea confers tremendous power on beasts and wizards alike.

Ursula K. Le Guin's dragons are also the object of adoration and reverence: 'I do not care what comes after; I have seen the dragons on the wind of morning', says Arren, another of the characters.

Magic is the essence of these wise and ancient beings who live on the West Reach of Earthsea. Humans must avoid looking them in the eyes so as not to fall victim to their tricks and spells, but that is easier to say than do. Among the inhabitants of Earthsea are Orm Embar, who dies helping the Archmage Ged, and Kalessin, who helps Ged and Arren return home after completing their dangerous mission in *The Farthest Shore*.